Y0-EFX-152

THE CRUSADES

by R. R. Sellman

Maps and Diagrams by the Author
and Pictures by
S. E. ELLACOTT

ROY PUBLISHERS NEW YORK

First published 9th June 1955

Reprinted 1957, 1960, 1961

NOTE TO SECOND EDITION

When this book first appeared the frontispiece showed the Knights Hospitaller of the Order of St. John of Jerusalem wearing Maltese crosses on their shields and surcoats. The Lieutenant Governor of Malta has informed us that the pictures and frescoes in the Palace, Malta, which was built by the Knights themselves, show them wearing the plain white cross on red ground when in armour and prepared for battle, though they wore the white eight-pointed Maltese cross on cloaks and robes in everyday life. The frontispiece has now been corrected accordingly, and so have the flags and pennants of the galley on page 28. A Knight and a Dame of the Order of St. John in civil attire, wearing the Maltese cross, are to be seen in *The Story of Nursing*, by J. M. Calder.

Editor.

PRINTED IN GREAT BRITAIN

CONTENTS

The Hospitallers at Arsouf

An Arab

INTRODUCTION

This book is intended as a brief account of the Crusading Movement, with the causes of its rise and decline and its effects on Western history.

The story of the Crusades is one chapter in the long history of contact and conflict between East and West, and it may still have lessons of value to our modern world. It is, too, a study in the mixture of human motives, and the way in which a noble idea may be used for ignoble ends. Finally, also, it shows how complicated questions of cause and effect in history may be, and how unwise are hasty and sweeping statements or interpretations which are purely romantic or purely cynical.

For its military details this book is greatly indebted to Professor Oman's *Art of War in the Middle Ages*, which is strongly recommended to any reader wishing to pursue the subject further.

R.R.S.

I CHRISTENDOM AND ISLAM

For thousands of years, while the empires of the Pharaohs, of the Assyrians and Persians, of Alexander and of Rome, rose and fell, Arabia remained an unconquered and unimportant backwater. Secure behind the desert barrier, its clans and tribes lived out their obscure lives as nomad herders or oasis cultivators. The hard conditions of their barren country, and their constant feuds and raiding, made them tough, warlike, and independent ; but also kept them poor and backward. Then suddenly, in the early seventh century, this remote and thinly-populated land gave birth to a Faith which changed the history of the world.

MUSLIM BELIEFS

Islam (which means submission to God's will), like Christianity, owed much to the Hebrews. From them it adopted the idea of the One True God, the universal Creator. It accepted Adam, Noah, Abraham, and Moses, as well as Christ, as prophets who had gradually made God better known to men ; and it asserted that Mohammed was the last and greatest prophet whose teachings eclipsed all that had gone before. From the Hebrews, too, Islam took its strict objection to eating pork, and to any form of picture or statue. It regarded Christians, with their crucifixes and images of the saints, as idolaters.

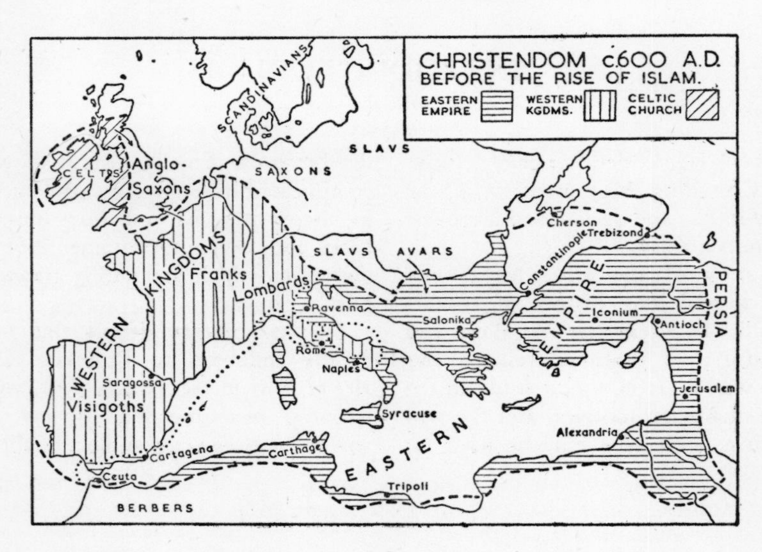

The Kaaba, Mecca

The ancient pre-Muslim cubic temple, cleared of its idols by Mohammed, which remains the centre of Muslim pilgrimage

Its creed was simple : " There is no God but Allah, and Mohammed is His prophet." Heaven, reserved for the Faithful, was a place of human delights, and Hell, for unbelievers, a place of torment. Prayer must be made towards Mecca five times a day, fast must be kept during daylight in the month of Ramadan, alms must be given to the poor and to holy men, and a pilgrimage must be made to Mecca. Like Christianity, Islam taught the brotherhood and equality of all within the Faith : and it gave the simple clansmen of Arabia a unifying force which they had never known before, which made their hardy and warlike qualities a menace to all outside the Muslim fold.

THE CONQUESTS OF ISLAM

Before Mohammed's death in 632 Islam had conquered Arabia, and his last instructions were to spread it beyond the land of its birth. Circumstances favoured this. The East Roman (or Byzantine) Empire and Persia had exhausted each other by a long and destructive war, and the East Roman provinces in North Africa and Syria had been made rebellious by taxation and religious persecution. In Spain the Visigothic conquerors who ruled this once-Roman province were feeble and unpopular, and Western Europe was divided.

In a series of rapid thrusts the warriors of Islam conquered Byzantine Syria and Egypt in a few years, and Persia and

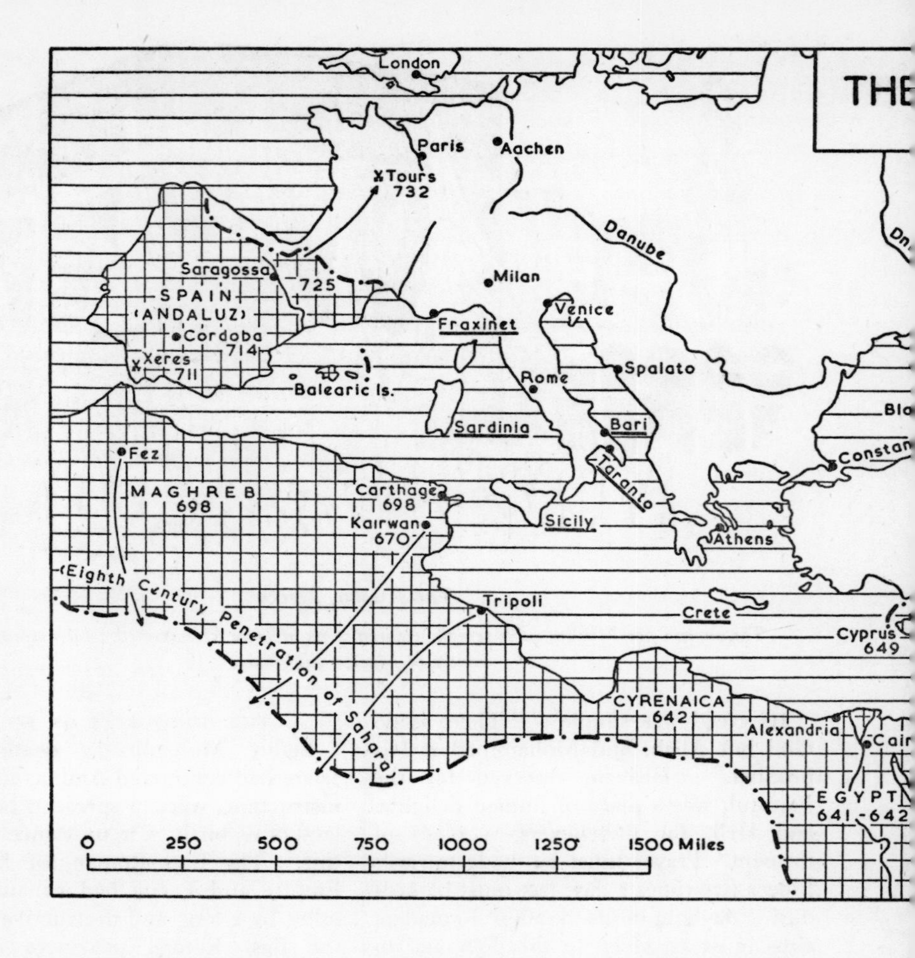

Cyprus in a few more. After a pause they overran the rest of North Africa before 700, and shortly afterwards nearly all Spain. By 730 their conquests stretched from the Pyrenees to the borders of India and China. Only the great victory of the French King Charles Martel at Tours in 732 stopped their progress and saved Western Christendom from collapse, while the Taurus Mountains checked their advance on Byzantine Asia Minor.

All over North Africa and Syria the church bells fell silent and were replaced by the muezzin's call to prayer. Christians were not too harshly treated, after the first rush of conquest, but they were subjected to special taxes and restrictions and many turned Muslim for its practical

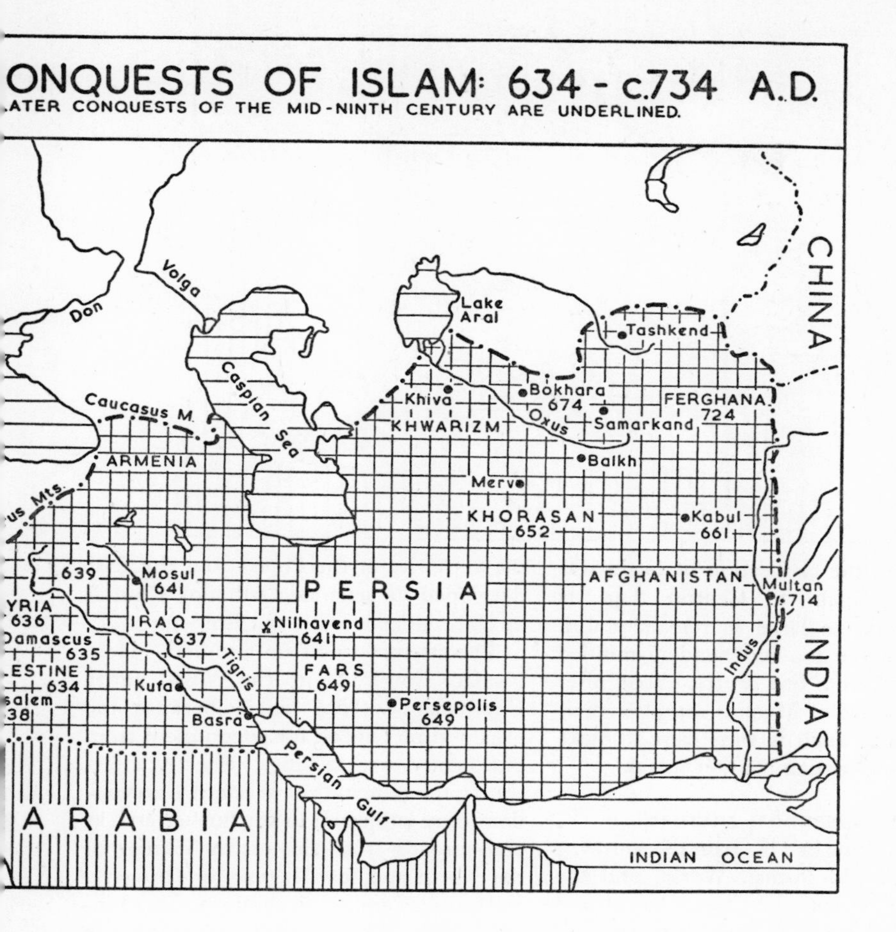

advantages. North Africa, which had been for centuries part of the Roman Empire and of Christendom, became finally a Muslim land. The Mediterranean, centre of the ancient Western world, became a frontier sea between two hostile Faiths and civilisations, and the Christian Holy Places of Jerusalem and Bethlehem fell under the Crescent of Islam.

MUSLIM CIVILISATION

The Arabs or Moors did not long remain primitive clansmen. With the help of the scholars and craftsmen of the conquered populations they built up a brilliant civilisation of their own which compared with that of Constantinople and was for centuries far ahead of that of the Western Europe of the Dark Ages.

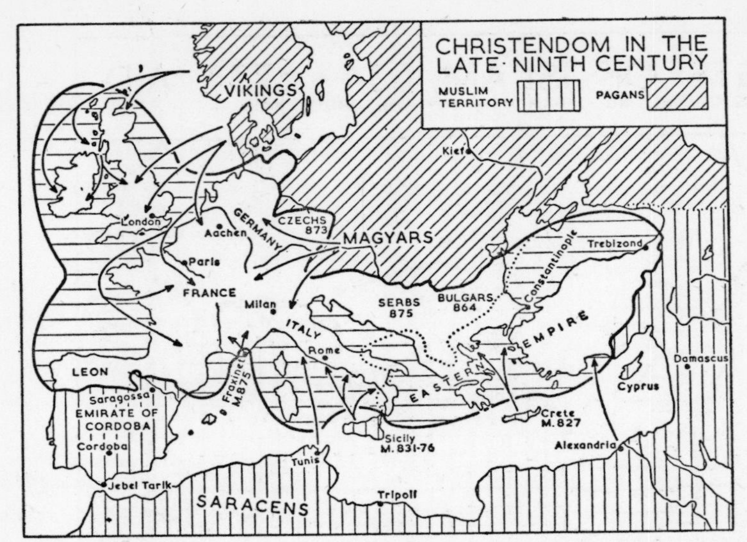

But though the civilisation of Islam was one from Spain to Central Asia its Empire was too large to remain a unit and its people too independent-minded to be ruled from one centre. Soon after the great wave of Muslim conquest divisions arose, which in time were to make possible a Christian counter-attack.

CHRISTENDOM DIVIDED

The Muslims had overrun the southern half of the old Roman World, and the rest was now split into two distinct and often hostile parts. The Eastern Empire, based on Constantinople, still survived and kept the Roman tradition of central government by one emperor : but the West—France, parts of Germany and Italy, and Britain—was a patchwork of little kingdoms ruled by descendants of the barbarian invaders. The West, except for the Celtic lands, looked to Rome as its religious centre and accepted the authority of the Pope : but the East developed its separate Orthodox Church in close alliance with the Emperor.

The attempt to set up a united " Holy Roman Empire " in the West under Charlemagne (800) failed, because the organisation needed for government from one centre was lacking. Shortly afterwards, the remnants of Western Christendom were subjected to yet further attacks and inroads from the pagan Vikings of the North and the Magyars of Hungary. In the ninth and tenth centuries Christendom was fighting desperately for its existence, ringed on all sides by pagan and Muslim enemies.

ELEVENTH CENTURY CHRISTIAN REVIVAL

Then, early in the eleventh century, came a momentous change. The Vikings and Magyars were converted to Christianity and ceased to be a menace, while the vigour of the Muslim assault on the Mediterranean coastlands and islands slackened with internal divisions and a more settled way of life. As the century progressed, Western Christendom emerged from the ordeal to find itself strengthened in body and spirit. In Sicily and South Italy, Norman adventurers drove out the Muslims and the remaining Byzantine governors and founded a realm whose sea-power challenged Islam on the Mediterranean. In North Italy, nominally part of the " Holy Roman Empire " but practically without a central government, cities like Venice, Genoa, and Pisa emerged as vigorous republics, looking to seaborne commerce for their prosperity. Genoa and Pisa drove the Moors from Sardinia in 1016, and in Spain the capture of Toledo in 1085 marked the final turn of the tide. But while this revival of Western strength was in progress, a new and disastrous blow fell on the East. From the steppelands of Asia Minor came the Seljuk Turks.

THE TURKS

The Turks, newly converted to Islam, had much in common with the original Arabs who had burst from Arabia four centuries before. A primitive, warlike, and fanatical people, organised to conquer but caring little for the arts of peace, they overran Persia and Syria and burst the Taurus barrier after the disastrous battle

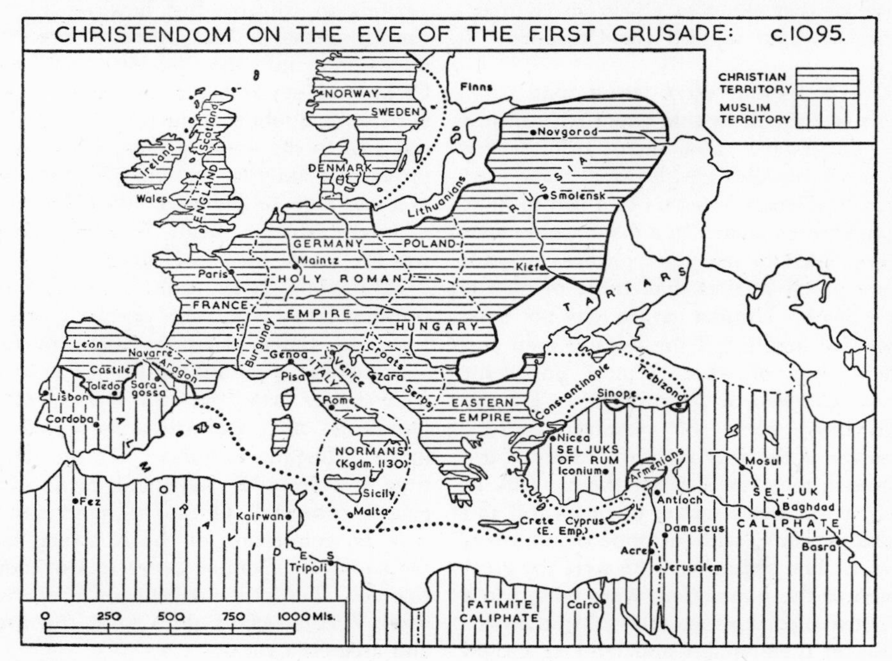

CHRISTENDOM ON THE EVE OF THE FIRST CRUSADE: c.1095.

of Manzikert (1071). Nearly all Asia Minor, main strength and recruiting-ground of the Eastern Empire, was conquered, ravaged, and reduced to a desert. Constantinople itself, the bulwark of Christendom, stood exposed to attack.

In centuries of civilised life the Arabs had learnt tolerance, and had allowed Christian pilgrims to visit Jerusalem without much interference. But the Turks were a different matter. Troops of pilgrims were held for ransom, enslaved, or slaughtered : and those who managed to return told tales which roused the indignation of Europe. The Turkish threat in the East came just when the West was feeling its new vigour and assurance, and the result was the beginning of that series of Christian counter-attacks which we call the Crusades.

THE CALL TO A HOLY WAR

It is difficult in this twentieth century to understand how men from every country of Western Europe responded readily in such numbers to a call to fight an unknown enemy in a distant unknown land, when to most the chances of gain were much smaller than those of misery and death. Human nature may not have changed much, but the lives of men and their ideas of what is most important have changed a great deal. To the ordinary people of eleventh century Europe ease and comfort meant little because they never knew them. Life in this world was a matter of much toil and little pleasure, without hope of improvement. The peasantry, who were the great mass of the population, were bound to a narrow and laborious life within the confines of their village and held in a rigid system which made them the serfs of their landlords and masters. To them, life was less dear and death less terrible, for only after death could they hope for better things. To the upper classes, knights and barons, war was the main business of life and the object of all their training. War against the Infidel offered an outlet for their energies without the moral doubts involved in fighting fellow-Christians, and to the lucky it offered conquest and enrichment with the full blessing of the Church. To the men of the trading cities, more modern in their outlook, the ports of the Holy Land were a great attraction, for through them passed the rich spice trade from the East which the Venetians and Genoese were anxious to control. But however much various personal and worldly interests might enter into the decision to take the Cross and set out for Palestine, there need be no doubt that the religious motive was real to the mass of men, and that it provided a unifying force to Christendom as it had done to Islam. To the Christian, as to the Muslim, death in a Holy War was the surest road to Heaven.

Meanwhile, circumstances in the East combined to favour the venture. After 1091 the Seljuk Empire began to fall apart, while Egypt and southern Palestine were under separate and hostile rule. Divisions and jealousies prevented a united Muslim resistance. At the same time the fleets of Italy and Sicily had gained command of the Mediterranean, and the conversion of the Magyars had reopened the Danube route to Constantinople. The way was already prepared when events occurred to raise the first and greatest Crusade.

II THE FIRST CRUSADE

ELEVENTH CENTURY WARFARE

The achievements, and the disasters, of the early Crusaders can only be understood in the light of the military methods and organisation of the period. At the end of the eleventh century the mailed horseman ruled the warfare of the west, outside the Viking lands, and England had seen his triumph over infantry at Hastings. No foot-soldiers could stand against the weight of a cavalry charge, and their use in campaigns had been reduced to that of camp-guards, servants, and general labourers in sieges. The complete supremacy of cavalry on the battlefield had been one of the reasons for the rise of feudalism, and the knight and baron were supreme in peace as well as war. In the West, battles were decided by the shock of opposing cavalry ; and tactics were a simple matter of charging in line against a similar enemy formation in the hope of breaking it up and causing a rout.

The mail-shirt, with its thousands of laboriously hammered small steel rings, gave excellent protection against sword cuts and arrows ; and a knight whose horse was brought down was more likely to be captured for ransom than killed or maimed. Infantry, however, could afford neither mail nor ransoms, and were often slaughtered wholesale. Campaigns were generally very brief, and little serious effort was made to organise supplies.

Mailed cavalry were very formidable, so long as they had only to deal with an enemy who could not avoid the weight of their charge and could not molest them from a safe distance. Their value was well understood by the Byzantines, and in 1094 the Eastern Emperor Alexius asked Pope Urban II to send him Western knights to help in his plan for reconquering Asia Minor now that the empire of the Seljuk Turks was breaking up. The result was more than he expected, but not quite what he wanted. His appeal came at a time when the possibility of war against the Muslims had already been in Western minds, and Pope Urban preached a Holy War which might incidentally bring some help to Constantinople but whose main object was the recovery of the Holy Land.

START OF THE FIRST CRUSADE

Minor preachers such as Peter the Hermit carried the call far and wide, and the response was amazing. Though no kings came forward, as in later Crusades, many barons and knights took the Cross, and a mass of humble folk, moved by many reasons from religious fervour to the hope of loot. Some ill-led and worse disciplined bands, including that of Peter the Hermit, moved off by the Danube route to Constantinople without waiting for the main force. Many never reached that city, for their pillaging in Hungary and Bulgaria caused clashes with the warlike peoples on the way Those who did were quickly shipped across the Straits and as quickly wiped out by the Turks at Nicaea. But this ill-starred venture had little connection with the real First Crusade.

TIME-CHART OF THE CRUSADING PERIOD:

DATE	EVENTS	BATTLES	CONQUEST	LOSS
	SELJUKS overrun Asia Minor	Manzikert 1071		
1080				
	Almoravides in Spain		Toledo 1085	
	Seljuk Empire disintegrates	Dorylaeum 1097	Edessa 1097	
	FIRST CRUSADE	Antioch 1098 Ascalon 1099	JERUSALEM 1099	
1100		Ramleh 1101, 1102	Acre 1104	
			Tripoli 1109	
			Akaba 1117	
1120		Hab 1119		
		Hazarth 1125	Tyre 1124	
	Rise of ZENGI of Mosul			
1140				EDESSA 1144
	SECOND CRUSADE		Lisbon 1147	Tell Basher 1150
			Ascalon 1153	
1160				
	Syrian Frank Invasions of Egypt			Akaba 1170
	Rise of SALADDIN			
1180				
		Tiberias 1187	CYPRUS 1190	KINGDOM OF JERUSALEM
	THIRD CRUSADE	Arsouf 1191	Palestine Coast recovered	
	Death of Saladdin	Alarcos 1195		
	Almohades in Spain			
1200	FOURTH CRUSADE		LATIN EMPIRE of Constantinople 1204	
	Albigensian Crusade			
	Children's Crusade	Las Navas de Tolosa 1212		
1220	FIFTH CRUSADE (EGYPT)			
	SIXTH CRUSADE		(Jerusalem temporarily recovered by treaty)	
1240			Valencia 1238	
	Charismians invade Syria	Gaza 1244		
	SEVENTH CRUSADE (EGYPT)	Mansourah 1250	Cadiz 1248	
1260	Mongols invade Syria			CONSTANTINOPLE 1261
	Crusade of St. Louis (Tunis) & Prince Edward		(Moors reduced to Granada 1266)	ANTIOCH 1268
1280				Markab 1285
	Mameluke Sultans extinguish Frankish holdings in Syria			TRIPOLI 1289
				ACRE 1291

By the end of 1096 the barons (mainly from France, West Germany, and Italy) and their following began to assemble at Constantinople. The Emperor Alexius, who had hoped for a manageable body of knights to enter his service, found instead a great mass of soldiery, without any recognised leader but determined to act on their own. He was anxious to get rid of them before they ate up all his supplies and proved a serious danger to Constantinople itself, but he also wanted to take advantage of any successes they might gain against the Turks. Their route to Palestine lay across the length of Asia Minor, and they could therefore still act as vanguard for a Greek re-conquest.

In May 1097 he ferried them across the Bosphorus, and they entered Turkish territory. In return for his assistance they had agreed to capture and hand over to him the Turkish capital of Nicaea, and only when this was done did the real march to Jerusalem begin. With it began too the entry into the unknown. Though the Greeks knew the road routes of their lost provinces, they could give little information on the existing condition of the country ; and much had happened since the Turkish hordes swept over it in 1071. Bridges had been broken, water supplies destroyed, population driven off or slain, and smiling cornlands reduced to a desert. Into this wilderness the Crusading hosts marched, to meet an enemy of whose methods of warfare they knew nothing.

THE BATTLE OF DORYLAEUM

Their first battle, at Dorylaeum, was nearly their last. Luckily, as it turned out, the army had divided into two parallel columns some seven miles apart, and it was on one only of these that the Turkish attack fell. It was bewilderingly unlike anything they had met in the West. The Turks were lightly armoured, mounted on swift horses, and used bows from horseback. Without any particular order they rode round and round the Christians, pouring in arrows from a safe distance and offering no opportunity for a charge. To modern eyes it was strangely like Red Indian tactics, and the knights had no long-range weapons. Any attempt at a cavalry charge would have been fatal : the Muslims would simply have made way for it and closed in behind. But to stand helpless under the rain of arrows would prove equally fatal in the long run. The knights, protected by their mail, suffered less than might be expected ; but their horses were dropping continually. Meanwhile the Turks entered the camp and slaughtered the infantry left there as a guard, and bewilderment at these new tactics began to verge on panic.

In the nick of time the situation was saved by the arrival of the other column, whose existence was apparently unknown to the enemy. Coming up unawares, they were able to form up and at last deliver their dreaded charge against the Muslim rear ; and impending disaster was turned to final victory. So complete was the rout that no further serious resistance was met with in Asia Minor : but had the Crusaders been in one mass, with no possibility of surprise or of using the only tactics they understood, it is unlikely that they would ever have passed Dorylaeum.

PERILS OF THE MARCH

Though Turkish armies gave little further trouble on the line of march, the lack of organisation in the Christian host brought further perils. Feudal armies had no adequate supply arrangements : they expected to feed men and horses from the country they passed through, and in the lands the Turk had wasted there was little food or forage. Infantry and horses suffered particularly from heat and lack of food, and many fell out or died on the route, while bands of Turkish horse-archers harassed the march and picked off stragglers. It was a much reduced host which eventually won through to Marash and Tarsus in Armenia, where they could find rest and supplies amongst a friendly Christian population. In spite of ignorance and lack of preparation, however, sufficient survived to carry on the march to Jerusalem. (It was very different with later forces which attempted a similar

The Crisis at Dorylaeum

The Walls of Antioch

route in 1101, with a similar disregard of difficulties, and were either completely wiped out or obliged to turn back with a tenth of their original numbers.)

Those who survived Dorylaeum had begun to learn the hard lesson that horse-archery, in open country, could only be countered by using infantry armed with the harder-hitting crossbow in combination with cavalry. But newcomers still tried to use Western tactics against an Eastern foe, and only realised their error when on the point of destruction.

THE SIEGE AND BATTLE OF ANTIOCH

In the autumn of 1097 the host moved into Syria, and shortly came up against the great walled city of Antioch, taken by the Turks from the Greeks only a few years before. The fortifications they found here were too strong for their feeble engines of attack, and they could not even blockade the place effectively. The siege dragged on for month after month, while supplies ran low, camp fevers took their toll, and the Muslims began to gather a relieving army. Here once again the Crusade might well have come to a disastrous end, if the Christians had been caught between the forces in the town and those coming up for its relief. But once more luck intervened at the crucial moment. A traitor was found in charge of one of the towers on the wall, who helped a body of Franks to climb up silently by night, massacre the unsuspecting defenders in the neighbouring towers, and seize sufficient of the ramparts to let the main army in. No sooner was the place taken than the advance guards of a huge Muslim army came in sight, and the Crusaders found themselves hemmed in within the fortress they had been for seven months besieging.

There was no choice but to come out and fight, for the alternative was starvation. So many horses had been lost, and so many knights dismounted, that infantry had to be used in the line of battle. Fortunately the lie of the ground was such that they were able to take a position between the city and the hills which could not be turned, and where the usual Turkish tactics of riding round and shooting arrows from a distance could not be employed. The Turks, like the Christians, had to form a line, and a line could be charged. A final advance of the remaining cavalry decided the day, for

The Escalade at Antioch

The Storming of Jerusalem

the Muslim horses were too light to stand against it and had no room to let it through and close in behind. Instead they used their superior speed to escape, and the battle was won. The Turks too had something to learn—that they must not give battle in a confined space where their special tactics were impossible.

THE CAPTURE OF JERUSALEM

The Battle of Antioch was fought in June 1098, and it was just a year before the Crusaders finally reached Jerusalem. Had they been concerned only with conquest, it would have been better to use Antioch as a firm base from which gradually to extend their power to the south and east. But to most of those present their real objective was the Holy City of Jerusalem, and so the host cut adrift from its only secure foothold and moved southwards through hostile territory, helped to some extent by ships with supplies which began to arrive off the coast. Fortunately there was little organised resistance. No important enemy forces appeared to block the way, and some strong places were found abandoned and others by-passed. Jerusalem was taken, after a month, by the use of siege-towers, though not before these had been so battered by the stone-throwing engines of the defence that the attack nearly failed. The religious thanksgiving and general massacre which followed throws a powerful light on the state of mind of men who had come so far and braved such dangers. They were Crusaders in a holy cause, but also soldiers made ruthless by the perils and hardships they had endured.

Not all the Franks who entered Syria took part in the capture of Jerusalem. Some remained at Antioch, and others instead moved eastwards across the Euphrates and founded the County of Edessa. By the end of 1099 Jerusalem, with its port of Jaffa, and Antioch and Edessa, were firmly in Christian hands but little else. The next essential step was to unite these scattered places by the conquest of Syria.

III THE CONQUEST OF SYRIA

THE GEOGRAPHY OF SYRIA

To understand the expansion and later decline of the Crusading States in Syria, it is necessary to have some idea of the geography of that country. Between the Mediterranean Sea and the desert there run four parallel but diverse belts of country : the coastal plain, the mountains, the great valley with the Jordan and other rivers, and the uplands of the eastern plateau. The coastal plain is very narrow, and sometimes disappears altogether where mountains overlook the sea, but it is of the first importance. Here lay at this period the trading ports through which passed much of the commerce between East and West, and it was the attraction of these ports which gave the Crusaders the naval co-operation of the Italian cities. Venice, Genoa, and Pisa, and to a lesser extent Amalfi and even Marseilles and Barcelona, were all anxious to have footholds here, and willing to assist in the capture and defence of these places in return for 'quarters' of their own within their walls.

Beyond the coast, however, they had no interest : and conquests inland were left to the barons and the feudal levies, helped occasionally by new arrivals from the West. The mountain chain a short distance inland was also of great importance, for only by the passes through it could the Crusaders attack the interior or the Muslims the coast. At the gaps in this chain grew up many of the famous Crusader castles, as guardians and as bases for further advance. Inland, between the great valley and the desert, lay the great Muslim centres of Aleppo and Damascus.

Syria as a whole, in the hands of anyone who, like the Crusaders, controlled the sea, would be defensively strong. Bounded by the desert on the east and south, and by the Euphrates and the Amanus Range on the north, it had natural boundaries which made it easy to defend. But the Crusaders never managed to reach these borders. That they conquered as much as they did was due, apart from Italian naval help, to the divisions and enmities which then existed between their Muslim neighbours of Aleppo, Mosul, Damascus, and Egypt.

THE LESSONS OF EASTERN WARFARE

After the capture of Jerusalem many of the host returned home. Others chose to remain and carve out new dominions for themselves in Syria. For some thirty years their efforts were almost uniformly successful, except where they neglected the most obvious precautions ; and sometimes battles were won even in spite of this. Egyptian armies, lacking the horse-archers of the Turks, were so easily defeated at Ascalon in 1099 that in 1101 Baldwin, the first King of Jerusalem, left his infantry behind and charged some 15,000 of them with little more than 200 knights. More by luck than judgment he gained a victory, but lost his entire force when he repeated the process with similar numbers in the following year. Having cut his way out of the mêlée and collected the reinforcements he should have waited for in the first place, he was able to beat off further Egyptian attacks by combining crossbowmen with cavalry.

When a balanced force was put in the field and the ground was well chosen, Crusaders frequently defeated much superior numbers. On the defensive, their crossbows carried farther and hit harder than horse-archery, while in the attack—if they could find something solid to aim at—the weight of their charge could overthrow a much larger force of light Muslim cavalry.

On the other side, the Battle of Harran in 1104 showed what might happen when lack of common sense played into Muslim hands. Here Bohemund of Antioch and Baldwin of Edessa were besieging the city when a relieving force appeared. They promptly charged it, over open country, the Muslims giving way for mile after mile, till they had to halt through sheer exhaustion and make camp. At this point, while tents were being pitched and all was in disorder, the Muslims charged in and captured the camp and the men inside it, leaving the rest foodless as well as exhausted. The demoralised infantry deserted, and the rest followed. Only the fact that the Turks were disputing over the spoil prevented pursuit and complete disaster.

The military lessons were clear enough for those who were willing to learn. With crossbowmen properly used in support of cavalry, with suitable ground, and with adequate supplies, the Crusaders could and did defeat much larger numbers with their superior weight and armour. But disaster could follow from the foolhardiness and indiscipline which so often marked the feudal host. Meanwhile, as

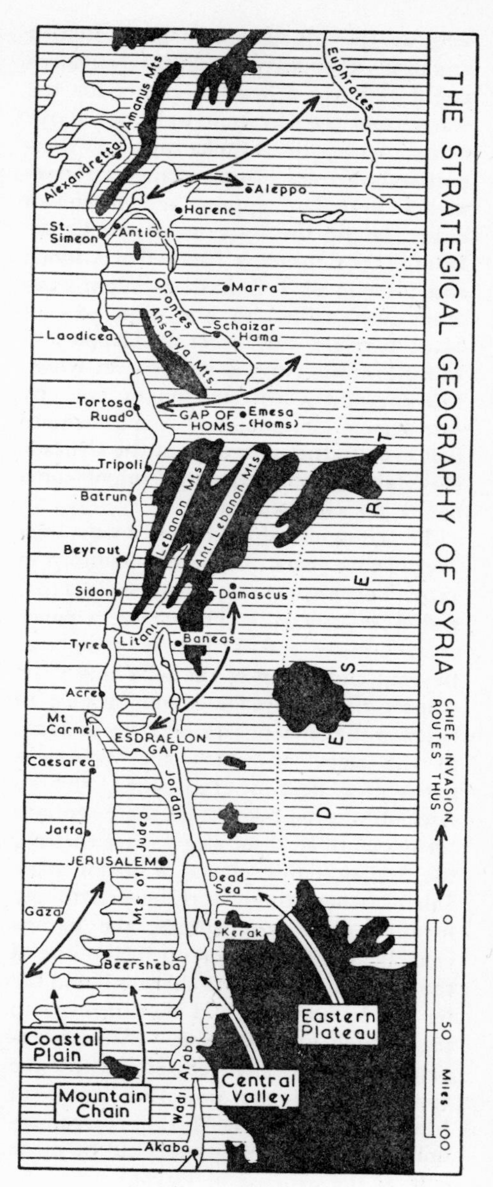

long as the Muslims remained divided amongst themselves, skilful alliances could help the Christian cause, for the warriors of the Crescent were not above siding with the Franks against their personal enemies. Such strange arrangements were, unhappily, not unknown either among the warriors of the Cross. In 1108 the Crusaders Tancred of Antioch and Joscelin of Tell Basher fought each other, each allied to one of a pair of Muslim rivals, the Emirs of Aleppo and Mosul! This curious struggle in which Muslim and Christian fought side by side against Christian and Muslim shows that even in the early days of the Crusading States personal quarrels might come before the common cause.

The conquest of the coastal towns took over twenty years. Caesarea was taken in 1101, Tortosa in 1102, Laodicea in 1103, and Acre in 1104. Then after a pause came Gibelet and Tripoli in 1109, and Beyrout and Sidon in the following year. Almost the last place of importance to fall was the ancient city of Tyre in 1124, to the siege of which the Venetians brought a fleet of 130 ships, though Ascalon was not taken from the Egyptians till 1153. In all these sieges, save the last, the Italian cities played a major part. Inland, where there were fewer strongly fortified places to capture, the barons consolidated their lands up to the line of the mountains. Only in the south and the far north, however, did they manage to push much beyond them. By 1127 expansion practically ceased with the appearance of the powerful Zengi of Mosul who began the Muslim reorganisation, and further progress could be made only at the expense of Egypt.

THE CRUSADING STATES

The states thus formed were four in number. Of these, much the most powerful and important was the Kingdom of Jerusalem, which held the coast from Beyrout southwards to the border of Egypt and stretched eastwards to, or beyond, the Jordan and the Dead Sea. A line of castles extended its territory down to the Gulf of Akaba, athwart the Muslim caravan route between Damascus and Cairo, and allowed its rulers to tax or interrupt this traffic. Only in the north-east, where it bordered the lands of the Emirs of Damascus, were its frontiers insecure, and here too was built a line of castles.

The King of Jerusalem claimed to be the overlord of the other three Christian rulers. The geography of Syria did not favour rule from one centre, and no attempt was made to incorporate the other lordships, but in time of crisis they generally supported each other. Kings of Jerusalem went to the help of Edessa in 1110 and Antioch in 1119, and twice temporarily took over the rule of Antioch till a new Prince could be chosen ; but in normal times the rulers of the other states were practically independent.

Though Jerusalem was the largest and strongest of the four, its military force was dangerously small for its defence. By stripping its garrisons it could put into battle some 800 knights and 1,000 or so heavy infantry, but its battles were often fought with yet smaller numbers. The largest army ever put in the field by all the states together, in 1183, amounted to only 1,300 knights and 15,000 foot. With such numbers it is not surprising that the complete conquest of Syria proved impossible : it is surprising that so much was in fact achieved.

North from Beyrout to beyond Tortosa stretched the County of Tripoli. This was the smallest and weakest of the states, and consisted of little more than the narrow coastal plain and a line of castles in the mountain passes. In the north it did not even hold the passes, but here lay an unexpected ally. The 'Assassins', a group of Muslim heretics who made common cause with the Franks against Aleppo and Damascus, defended their mountain fastnesses against all comers but gave no trouble in the plain. Their chiet, the "Old Man of the Mountain," their use of hashish, and their skill in stealthy murder, have made them a legend. Though Tripoli never managed to expand across the mountains, it held its border there with the help of the Assassins for over two hundred years.

The Principality of Antioch had no such frontiers. Between it and the unconquerable Muslim stronghold of Aleppo lay a disputed land, over which the border varied with the fortunes of war. Antioch alone was secure behind the Byzantine walls which baffled the Crusaders in 1097, and it was never taken till the final collapse in 1268. Elsewhere, castles and towns changed hands repeatedly ; and in course of time the borders of the Principality contracted towards the capital.

The County of Edessa was even more precarious, since in the first flush of success it was pushed far into Mesopotamia over an area surrounded by Muslims on three sides and lacking any defensible frontier. Very few Crusaders settled here, but it had something the

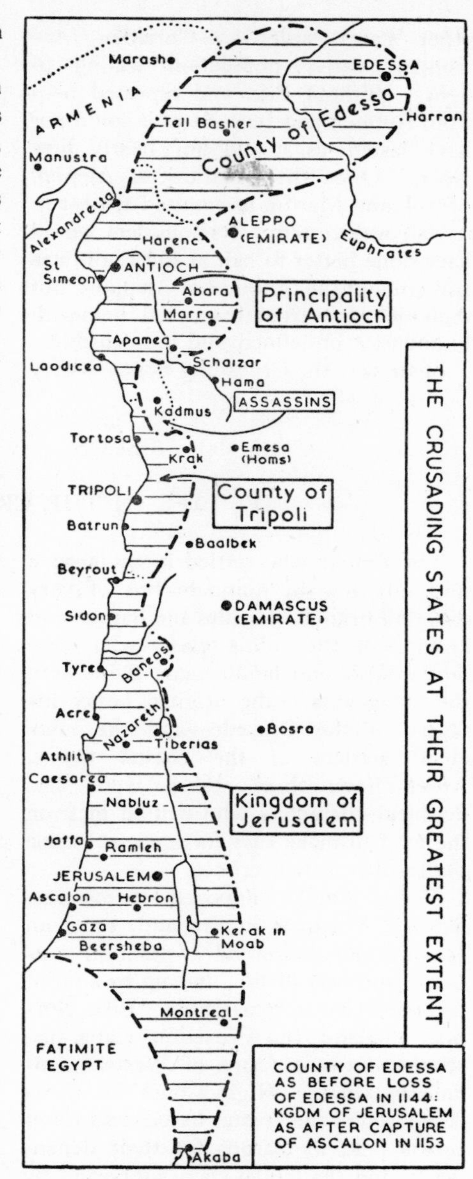

THE CRUSADING STATES AT THEIR GREATEST EXTENT

other states lacked—a Christian (Armenian) native population willing to fight. Without this, and repeated help from Antioch and Jerusalem, it could not have lasted as it did for nearly fifty years. Once the Muslims of Aleppo, Mosul, and Mardin had united against it, its fall was certain. Its founders would have done better to halt at the Euphrates and attempt the conquest of Aleppo ; but their rash eastwards advance left them with boundaries undefined and indefensible.

Such were the Crusading States as they emerged in the quarter-century after the First Crusade, with their feudal ruling class drawn haphazard from the west and imposed upon a far larger and partly Muslim native population, and their trading ports colonised by the merchants of Italy. Here two civilisations and two religions met and existed side by side, and here a European minority found itself in contact with a strange people and a strange way of life. The Franks made a great difference to Syria, but Syria also had its effect on the Franks.

IV LIFE IN THE CRUSADING STATES

The Franks who settled in Syria were not only few in numbers but of very different origins. Besides the barons and knights of the ruling class, who were feudal lords and landowners, there were the ' sergeants '—the original heavy infantry of the Crusade—and the merchant settlers of the coastal towns. Apart from these, there were also doubtful characters who drifted in from the west to make easy fortunes or escape the results of their crimes.

These Franks imposed themselves, like the Normans in England, upon an existing population of a different language and way of life, and up to a point the parallel was remarkable. Like Norman England, the Crusading states had all the outward forms of Western feudalism, with a High Court or Curia composed of the greater barons and lesser courts held by barons for their dependents, and the feudal class supported by the labour and tribute of the peasants on their ' manors '. The townsmen, specially privileged like those of the chartered towns of the west, ran their own affairs with burgess courts, and special tribunals were set up for matters of trade and seafaring which administered the ' Law Merchant ' of Medieval Europe.

EASTERN INFLUENCES

But beneath the outward Western forms, and the tournaments and heraldry of knighthood, there were notable differences. The Normans in England had no change of climate to consider, and had nothing to learn from their Saxon peasantry ; but the Franks in Syria soon began to adopt from the inhabitants a new way of life which was more civilised and more suited to the country. When they were not fighting, they shed their armour and wore the flowing robes and turbans of the East, and their ladies even

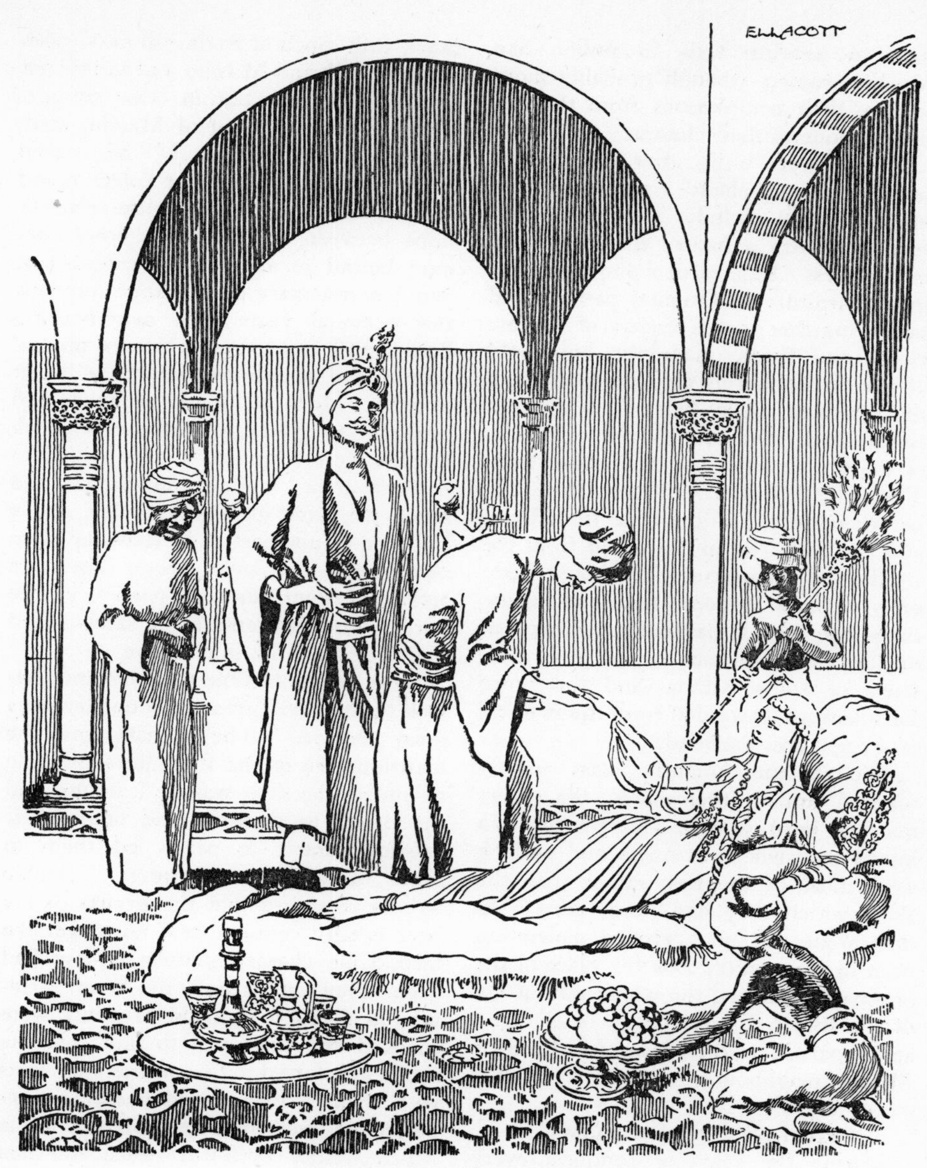

A Syrian-Frankish Household

took to wearing veils in public like Muslim women—though probably more to save their complexions from the sun than to conceal their charms.

Houses were built, after the Eastern fashion, round shady courtyards with fountains to exclude the heat, and furnished with a luxury then unknown in the West. Rich carpets and hangings, inlaid furniture of Oriental pattern, and baths, together with a variety of delicate cloths and foods, made the household of the Syrian baron very different from the bare and smoky hall of his Western counterpart. Syria itself produced many of these luxuries : silk cloth came from Tripoli and Antioch, carpets from Tiberias, pottery and fine glass from Tyre, and the best steel in the world from the smithies of Damascus. The countryside grew oranges, lemons, figs, and sugar-cane—the last a particular delicacy to mediæval Europeans—while the products of India, China, and the Spice Islands were forwarded from the markets of Aleppo and Baghdad.

Though the knightly class mostly married among themselves, the others married local women and produced a mixed race whose manners and outlook were those of the East rather than the West which they had never seen. As time went by and a second generation born in the country took the place of the original Crusaders, the whole way of life of the Syrian Franks began to change ; and in particular, their relations with their Muslim neighbours.

CONTACTS WITH MUSLIMS

During the years of conquest every Infidel was an enemy : but when peace came, with much of Syria still in Muslim hands, Frank and Muslim had to live not only side by side but in close contact. Only by fair treatment of Muslim merchants could the trade of the coastal cities (and the revenue the rulers raised from it) be maintained, and close relationships between merchants on both sides were bound to arise. The rulers, too, found it necessary to exchange missions and personal visits with neighbouring Emirs, and from these contacts mutual respect and sometimes friendship began to grow. Much of the old prejudice had been due to ignorance, and the Frankish knights were surprised and delighted to find that their ' infidel ' counterparts had much the same ideas of chivalry, and a standard of manners and behaviour often better than their own. Soon they were arranging joint hunting parties in the border districts, and both sides found that they had a lot in common.

So in course of time the lives and outlook of the Frankish settlers underwent a great change. The climate and the luxurious life of the East did something to undermine their warlike leanings, and the desire to preserve and enjoy their existing estates in peace led them to avoid unnecessary fighting. Arabic writers remarked that the Franks of the later twelfth century were no longer the formidable characters their fathers had been. Newcomers from the West, arriving full of zeal to fight the Muslims, were shocked and dismayed to find that the settlers preferred to live on friendly terms with them. They could hardly be expected to welcome new pilgrim hosts which would break the peace and then return to the West, leaving them and their estates to bear the brunt of a Muslim counter-attack.

SETTLERS AND NEWCOMERS

This division between settlers and newcomers was to ruin the Second Crusade and divide Christian counsels throughout the rest of the history of the Crusading States. It was also the most serious bar to understanding between Christians and Muslims. The memoirs of the Emir Ousama of Schaizar throw an interesting light on this from the other side. He travelled much through the Kingdom of Jerusalem, and was generally on friendly terms with the settled Christians, though he felt obliged to call the curses of Allah upon them in his writings to show that he was still a good Muslim. The Templars of Jerusalem (see page 26) knew him well, and allowed him to pray in their church. One day a knight rushed up and rudely turned Ousama's face to the east instead of to Mecca, saying, " This is how to pray ! " The others hustled him out and apologised, explaining that he was a newcomer who had only just arrived and did not know the customs of the country. " It is always those who have recently arrived," says Ousama, " who show themselves more inhuman than those who have been established among us and become acquainted with Muslim ways."

DANGER AND UNCERTAINTY

But beneath the pomp and glitter of chivalry, and the luxury of Oriental life, there was always an uneasiness and uncertainty among the Syrian Franks. Diseases unknown to Europe took a heavy toll, especially among children, and this was particularly serious in a feudal society where the lack of an heir at a critical moment might prove disastrous. Not only were the settlers few in the beginning, but they failed to maintain their numbers. Meanwhile around and amongst them lay a much larger native population, some Muslim, and even the Syrian Christians hostile to the Latin Church imposed by the West. On the borders, never far away, lay the Muslim hosts, which in spite of personal friendships might at any time unite to overwhelm this precarious structure ; and within the borders there was always the danger of poison or the assassin's knife. The feudal nobility alone could not long have held the Crusading States in these conditions. That they survived as long as they did was largely due to the two great Military Orders, the Knights Hospitallers and Templars.

V THE MILITARY ORDERS

Not long after the First Crusade, while the Christian power in Syria was still expanding, there emerged the two great Military Orders. The Templars started as a small band of knights pledged to patrol the roads and protect pilgrims to Jerusalem, and in 1118 they were given a headquarters near the Temple from which they took their name. The Hospitallers could trace their origin back to the early eleventh century, when a hospital for pilgrims was opened in Jerusalem, but they did not become a fighting body till some years after the Templars. Both Orders, as finally organised, were a curious combination of the monastic and the knightly life. Their members took the religious vows of poverty, chastity, and obedience, but their monasteries were castles and their main duty the protection of the Holy Land by force of arms.

A Knight-Templar

The Templar and Hospitaller could combine the religious life with the life of action, and this opportunity was so attractive to the mind of twelfth-century Europe that their numbers rapidly grew and their organisation spread from Syria to the West. Under the Grand Master and his Council, with the Seneschal and Marshal charged with the supply of warlike equipment and horses, the Templars had Provincial Commanders for each of the Crusading States except Edessa (which disappeared too early from the scene). Soon, as the Order grew in popularity and repute, more provinces were organised in England, France, Portugal, Spain, Italy, and Hungary, and houses were established in the West as places of recruitment for new members and of retirement foi knights whose fighting days were done. As soldiers, the heads of these houses were known not as abbots but as 'Commanders'. The Hospitallers had a similar organisation, and both were distinguished by the Cross on their mantles—the Templars red on white, the Hospitallers white on red. (The Maltese cross was adopted later in Malta, and only for civil dress).

MILITARY VALUE OF THE ORDERS

In Syria the Orders did not consist only of knights, for as a balanced fighting force they had to have infantry as well. Each knight normally had a squire who served an apprenticeship to knighthood, and a number of 'sergeants' or serving brothers of lower degree was maintained by each Order as heavy infantry. Both too employed a force of light-armed horse-archers on the Turkish model, as scouts and skirmishers.

The Orders provided something that the Crusading States badly needed—a supply of new blood from the West to make up for the lack of numbers, and later of fighting power, of the settled baronage. As Orders they became very wealthy, but the individual knight had no estates to lose and no personal reasons for avoiding warfare. In course of time, therefore, the defence of the Crusading States fell increasingly into their hands. Castles were built by them, or made over to them, on the borders in the places of greatest danger, and the Syrian Franks could not have survived the disasters of 1187 without their aid.

Inevitably jealousies arose between them and the feudal knights and barons, for in the later years of the Crusading States the Orders were always ready for fighting while the barons were mostly anxious to avoid it. In time, too, jealousies arose between the two Orders, which played their part in the divisions which were the curse of the later history of the Syrian Franks.

With the fall of Jerusalem to Saladin in 1187 both transferred their headquarters to Acre, where they remained till this last Syrian foothold was lost in 1291. Thence they retired to Cyprus, still in Christian hands, to carry on the fight. Soon afterwards, in 1312, the Order of the Temple came to an inglorious end. Its wealth in the West had attracted the greed of kings; and on charges of immorality which were exaggerated or invented it was suppressed and its property seized—much as that of the English monasteries was later taken by Henry VIII.

SURVIVAL OF THE HOSPITALLERS

But the Hospitallers continued their active and honourable career for centuries. In 1309 they captured Rhodes, and held it against the Turk for over two centuries. Driven out in 1522, they found a new home in Malta, which they made one of the strongest fortresses in Europe and defended against the most desperate Muslim assaults. For years the galleys of St. John carried on the naval war against the Turk and the Barbary pirates of North Africa, until both sides gradually relaxed their efforts. Malta remained in the hands of the Hospitallers till 1798, when the last Grand Master surrendered it to Napoleon and he in turn was ousted two years later by the British. A remarkable history had sprung from the little hospital founded about 1020 in Jerusalem, and its story is not yet done. Its military functions finished, the

A Galley of the Knights of Malta

Order was revived on the original lines as a medical and charitable organisation, and its members today still bear the white cross of the ancient knights. (See Calder, *The Story of Nursing*.)

THE TEUTONIC KNIGHTS

A third Order, important in European history but less so in that of Syria, arose from the German hospital which existed in Jerusalem from 1128 to 1187 and was refounded at Acre in 1191. Round about 1200 this also developed into a Military Order, wearing a white mantle with a black cross. Though its headquarters remained at Acre till 1291, its activities were mainly on the shores of the Baltic. These Teutonic knights, as they came to be known from their German origin, began in the early thirteenth century the conquest of East Prussia and what is now Estonia and Latvia from the pagan Lithuanians. Like many of the later 'Crusades', this had nothing to do with fighting Islam, and its story is outside the main theme of this book. It extended the borders of Christendom by the sword, and left these Baltic Provinces with a German ruling class which endured until 1945. The Order itself ruled them until 1525, when the last Grand Master dissolved it and made himself instead Grand Duke. When the Lithuanians were converted to Christianity in the fifteenth century, the Teutonic knights lost their last claim to be Crusaders; and their importance in history is mainly in the part they played in the eastward drive of the Germans against the Slavs.

There was also one little known but

interesting English Order, the Knights of St. Thomas of Acre, who wore a cross of red and white. Established in 1231 in imitation of the Templars, they migrated with them to Cyprus in 1291 and continued there till nearly the end of the fourteenth century.

Amidst the general uncertainty of the Frankish position in Syria, the Templars and Hospitallers of the mid-twelfth century stood out as a vigorous, reliable, and well-organised fighting force. With the decline in Crusading power and the recovery of Islam, their efforts were soon to be needed to save the Crusading States from complete extinction.

VI THE MUSLIM RECOVERY

After the appearance of Zengi of Mosul in 1127, who made himself master of Aleppo in the following year, Frankish progress practically ceased ; and before long the Muslim counter-attack began. The remote Christian outpost of Edessa was captured, finally, in 1144, and the remaining fragments of the county vanished in a few more years. The early fall of Edessa had been inevitable, and was of no great importance in itself, but the news of it made a sensation in the West and led to the Second Crusade.

THE SECOND CRUSADE IN ASIA MINOR

In 1148 King Louis VII of France and the Emperor Conrad of Germany took the Cross in person, and led their armies overland to Constantinople. Their intention was to follow the route of the First Crusade through Asia Minor, but they found this impossible. Though in one respect the task should have been easier, since the Greeks had profited by the First Crusade to recover western Asia Minor and most of the southern coast, yet the usual crusading rashness and lack of forethought brought disaster. The Turks had wasted a broad belt of 'scorched earth' on the Byzantine border, and no adequate supplies were taken to allow for this, while the armies were hampered by hordes of camp-followers who ate but could not fight. No attempt was made to learn from earlier disasters, or to adopt new tactics to meet those of the Turks. Even the climate was ignored, and Louis tried to take his army through mountain passes in the depth of winter.

Conrad, after a quarrel with the Greeks, started on the road straight across Asia Minor by Iconium, taking a week's food for a journey of more than a month (Map, p. 30) His men were soon starving, and when the Turks attacked them they had no crossbowmen and their horses were too weak and weary to charge. In a running fight they were chased back to Nicaea, and arrived in such a condition that most of them gave up and drifted back to Germany. Conrad took ship for Palestine and reached Acre, but brought with him only a tiny fraction of the host with which he had set out.

King Louis was wiser, but still not wise enough. He took a route which kept him in Greek territory, where some supplies could be found, and though the Turks attacked him there his men were fit enough to fight their way through.

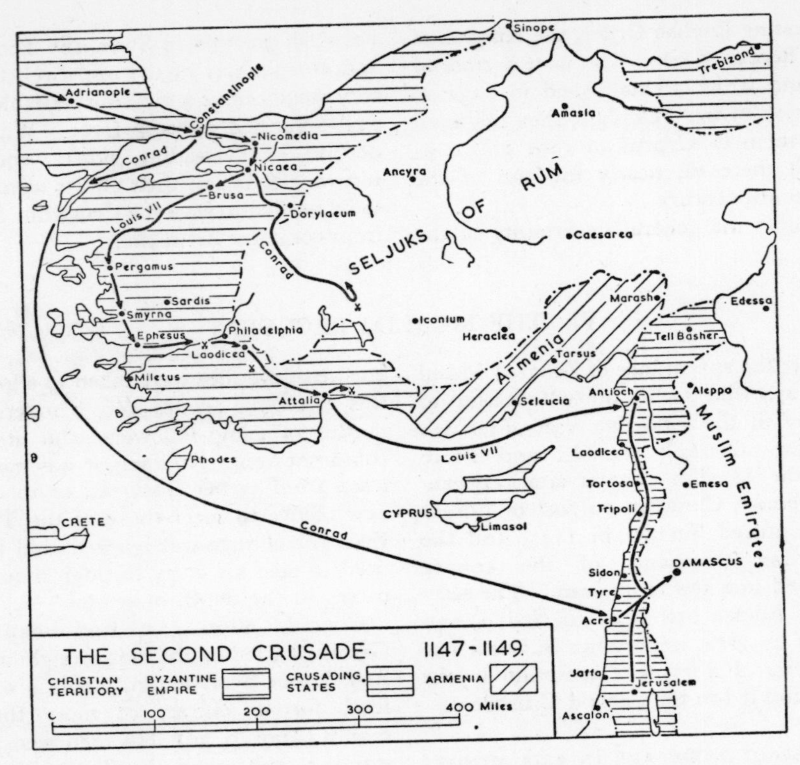

But nevertheless food ran short. The Greeks could not or would not provide all the host required ; and the indiscipline of the vanguard, who ignored their orders to hold a pass, allowed the convoys to be ambushed and much of the remaining stores lost. Louis then gave the command to the Master of the Templars who happened to be with him, and this veteran brought the host safely to Attalia.

Here supplies failed completely. The host could get no farther by land, and there were ships for only a few. Louis and his knights went off to Antioch by sea, and abandoned the infantry to their fate. Most died of disease and starvation : some made a desperate attempt to cut their way through and were wiped out. Others in despair turned Muslim rather than starve. Louis, like Conrad, brought only a fraction of his army through to Palestine.

FAILURE OF THE SECOND CRUSADE

Though the force which arrived in Syria was much less than had been hoped for, it was still large enough to give the Franks a new chance to attack before Muslim power became too strong. The

The Second Crusade in Asia Minor

plan decided on in 1149 was to capture Damascus, and drive a wedge between Zengi and Egypt. It was a good scheme, and promised to delay and perhaps prevent the threatened Muslim union : but the difference of view between the newcomers and the settled Franks wrecked it. The King of Jerusalem hung back and then abandoned the siege : either because he was jealous of the proposal to give Damascus to a newcomer or because, as the Muslims relate, the Emir offered to restore the castle of Baneas if he departed and threatened to deliver the city to Zengi if he did not. For whatever reason, he called off his forces and left : and the pilgrims from the West gave up the campaign in disgust. The chance of carrying the Frankish frontier to the desert had been thrown away, and there was never to be another.

Instead, the King of Jerusalem set out on a series of adventures against Egypt. Even though he was temporarily successful, it was futile to try to master Egypt while Damascus was unconquered and his own frontiers were unsafe. Zengi's death gave some temporary respite, but before long the clouds again gathered. By 1183 the famous Saladin had united all the Muslim lands from Egypt to Mesopotamia, and the end of the Kingdom of Jerusalem was in sight.

SALADIN (*or* SALADDIN, SALA-UD-DIN)

After some raids on the borders and the capture of a few outlying places, Saladin determined in 1187 on striking at the heart of the Kingdom of Jerusalem with all the force he could muster. The Franks, realising that this was the hour of crisis, also raised every available man. The feudal knights, the Templars and Hospitallers, and the infantry contingents of the cities, gathered behind the True Cross and set out to meet the invasion. Castles and towns were stripped of their garrisons, and all was staked on one throw. This policy was probably wise, for one great force had more chance of success than several small ones, but it meant that failure would be final. There were no reserves.

Saladin had crossed the border near the Sea of Galilee, and taken the town of Tiberias, but its castle still held out. The Frankish host gathered near Nazareth, and a council of war was held. There were two possible plans : to wait in a good position, with abundant water and supplies, till Saladin was forced by lack of either to retreat or attack (which might first mean the loss of the castle of Tiberias) : or to advance against him across the intervening wilderness and give battle at once. It was the heat of summer, and whichever army marched to battle would be thirsty and weary before a blow was struck.

THE BATTLE OF TIBERIAS

As often happened, those who advised prudence were called cowards and traitors : and it was decided to leave the stores behind and march straightway on Tiberias. This decision proved the ruin of the Kingdom of Jerusalem. No sooner had the great straggling column begun its march than the horse-archers appeared to harass and delay it ; and long before they had reached either Tiberias or a supply of water the Templar rearguard was compelled to halt to defend itself. To avoid losing touch the rest of

Disaster at Tiberias

Saladin

the army also halted, and then encamped, without water for horse or man and with little food. To make matters worse the Turkish archers kept up a harassing fire throughout the night, and set light to the dry grass around the camp.

When next day the King ranged the host for battle, the infantry declared that they were dying of thirst and could not fight. They deserted to a neighbouring hill and left the cavalry defenceless against the Turkish bowmen. This made the situation hopeless. Some of the horsemen cut their way out with a desperate charge and escaped, but the rest were encircled by the Muslim swarms and engulfed, while the infantry threw down their weapons and surrendered. The King, the Master of the Hospitallers, many barons, and hundreds of knights were taken captive : and hundreds of Templars and Hospitallers were immediately slaughtered.

This battle need never have been fought. Had wiser counsels prevailed, Saladin must either have retreated or have attacked the Franks in their chosen position while they were fresh and his forces weary. In either case the Kingdom would, for the time, have been saved. Even the march undertaken need not have been disastrous had there been more care about water and supplies ; and had the Franks been able to give battle in a fit condition they might well have caught Saladin with his back to the Jordan and pushed his forces into the river with the weight of their charge. But the damage was now done. Rashness and mismanagement had thrown away the last chance the Syrian Franks were to have of meeting the Muslims on anything like equal terms.

LOSS OF THE KINGDOM OF JERUSALEM

After this the Kingdom of Jerusalem collapsed like a house of cards. Towns and castles were taken with ease, or opened their gates for lack of defenders. Jerusalem itself fell in a few days, and two melancholy columns of Christians left its gates—those who could find a ransom departing to the coast, and the rest into captivity. The outlying castles of Kerak and Montreal, which had not been left ungarrisoned like the rest, held out longer ; but elsewhere every place of importance in the Kingdom except Tyre fell promptly into the hands of Saladin.

The disaster was much more crushing than the loss of Edessa. This time the

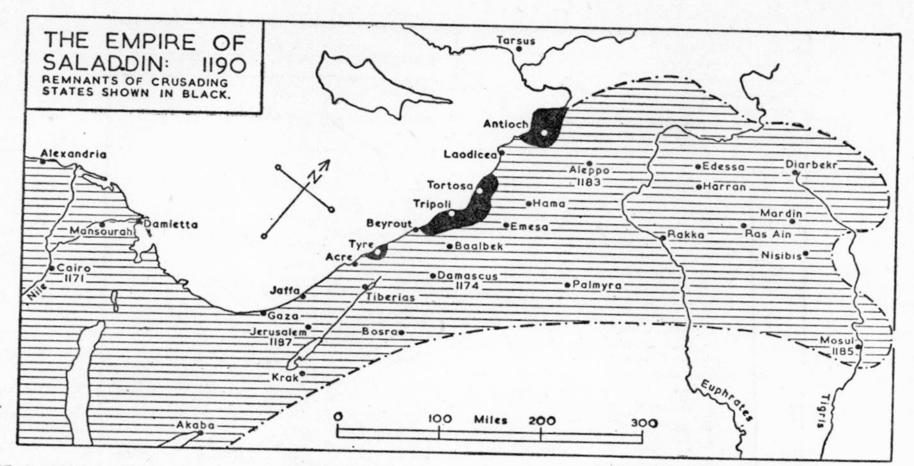

Holy Places for which the first Crusaders had fought were once more subject to Islam, and the whole structure of the Crusading States had been shattered. Only by vigorous and immediate help from the West could something be salvaged from the wreck, and this was not long in coming.

VII THE THIRD CRUSADE

A year after the disaster of Tiberias, Saladin released King Guy of Jerusalem on his promise not to renew the war. Like Harold of Wessex after his oath to William, Guy took the view that "a forced oath is not binding," and the clergy absolved him from keeping his promise on the ground that an oath made to an infidel did not count. Whatever we may think of the morality of this, we must admire the courage with which Guy set about the apparently hopeless task of retrieving the results of his earlier rashness. As the first fresh Crusaders began to arrive at Tyre from the West, he gradually gathered a new army and in 1189 once more challenged Saladin by laying siege to Acre. When Saladin arrived with a relieving force a battle took place in which the Franks were worsted, but not dislodged. The Muslims had a healthy dread of attacking Westeners when they were well posted and plentifully supplied with crossbows, and the siege continued. Meanwhile powerful forces were collecting in Europe for the recovery of the Holy Land.

BARBAROSSA

This time three leading monarchs took the Cross—Richard I of England, Philip Augustus of France, and the Emperor Frederick I (Barbarossa) of Germany. Only the last attempted the land route

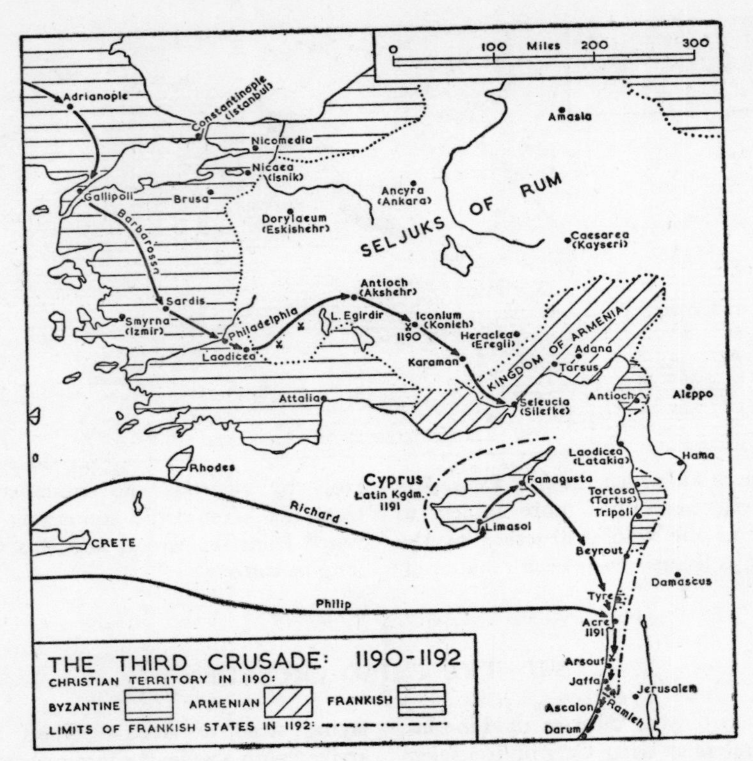

through Asia Minor which had proved so disastrous in the past. Barbarossa, a hardened campaigner, followed part of the route of Louis VII through Greek territory and then struck boldly inland towards Iconium. Fierce fighting followed ; but though the horses suffered severely the mail coats were effective, and the advance, though harassed, could not be halted. Before starvation could do its usual work, Frederick reached and captured the Turkish capital of Iconium, and supplied his army from the Turkish stores. This caused such consternation to the Sultan that he offered the German host unmolested passage for the rest of their journey, if they would leave at once. The terms were accepted, and the last great host to try the overland route to Syria got through safely to Antioch. Frederick himself, however, after braving all the perils of battle and starvation, was drowned while bathing in a river.

KING RICHARD'S CAMPAIGN

Richard and Philip Augustus both went by sea. The Mediterranean route was now so well known, and the West so much better equipped with shipping, that a direct sea-route for armies was possible :

and the perils and wastage of a Mediterranean voyage were far less formidable than those of the long march. Richard conquered Cyprus on the way, which he afterwards sold to King Guy, and both arrived safely at Acre and joined the siege.

The siege of Acre was a desperate business. It had been begun by Guy in the summer of 1189, and it dragged on for two years while Saladin hovered near by and often attacked the Crusaders' camp and lines. But no fortress can hold out for ever, and the Christian host was now too large to be driven off. Completely blockaded by land and sea, and despairing of relief, the garrison at last surrendered.

But Saladin refused all offers of a treaty. He evidently hoped that once the Crusaders broke camp and moved into the open their own errors would lead them to disaster, as at Tiberias. When the walls of Acre had been repaired, and the Muslim garrison beheaded for lack of ransom, it was decided to march on Jerusalem. Philip Augustus had by this time left for France, the opportunity of stirring up trouble in Richard's Norman dominions while Richard was still in Palestine proving more attractive than further Crusading, and the English king was left in sole command.

Whatever his shortcomings as a king, as a warrior Richard was superb. He not only loved fighting but, which was much rarer, understood it. Though he had no previous experience in Eastern warfare, he had enough sense and originality of mind to learn about Muslim tactics and the way to meet them, and enough generalship to pick the only practicable

Richard I

route for his march. As far as Jaffa, from which there is a good road to Jerusalem, he intended to march along the coast. This not only allowed the ships to keep touch, but also protected one flank of the army and prevented the favourite Muslim tactic of encirclement. As soon as the column moved it must expect attack ; and it had therefore to be marshalled in battle order, to carry out the most dangerous manœuvre of a flank march across the enemy's front. Horses and mules were scarce, so some of the infantry had to take their turn at carrying the tents and stores. These, who were too burdened to defend themselves, marched next to the sea. Covering them were the cavalry, and protecting the whole front was a solid line of crossbowmen. The veteran Templars and Hospitallers supplied the van and rearguard in turn, and Richard himself moved continually along the lines to see that all was in order and no gaps developed. Haste would have been fatal, for it was still August and the foot were heavily burdened. The march therefore went slowly and by easy stages, with frequent days of rest. All reasonable precautions were taken, and nothing left to chance.

THE BATTLE OF ARSOUF

Saladin's skirmishers hung about the column like a swarm of mosquitoes, trying by their archery to goad the knights into a charge which would break the ranks and make possible an assault by the main Turkish force : but it was of no avail. Patience and discipline and firm leadership, so often lacking in Frankish armies, kept the ranks solid and impenetrable. Realising that these tactics would never prevent the Crusaders reaching Jaffa, Saladin decided to try conclusions with a general attack near Arsouf, where thick woodland close to the shore gave cover for a sudden swoop. Saladin's plan, as at Tiberias, was to attack the rearguard and force it to halt and turn, in the hope of causing a break in the column into which his horsemen could charge. Richard, with a general's eye for ground, had expected the attack and foreseen the form it was likely to take. He gave strict orders that, whatever happened, there was to be no breaking of the lines to charge until the signal was given. It was essential that the charge, when it came, should be general, and that it should not come until the enemy was so closely engaged that he could not avoid it.

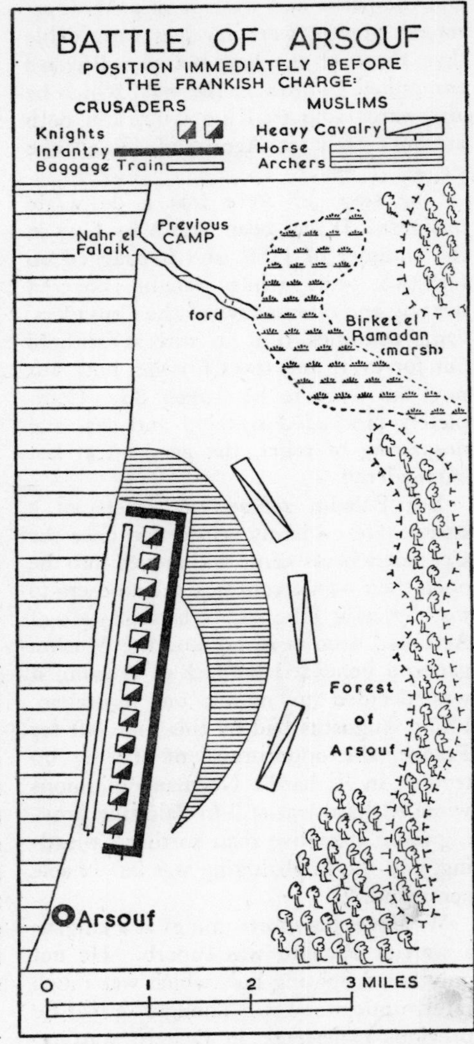

The devoted Hospitallers held the rear this day, and suffered the brunt of Muslim archery from two directions, losing many horses but keeping their discipline. The six trumpets of Richard's signal were never sounded, however, for when he was about to give the order the Hospitallers at last could stand it no longer and broke out against their tormentors. But their hours of endurance had borne fruit. The charge was taken up all along the line, and Richard joined in with the centre and the van. The Turks, as their own chroniclers admit, were taken utterly by surprise and panicked. Even then discipline was strong enough to halt the charge, reform, and charge again and a third time, till the Muslim host was driven completely from the field. No foolhardy pursuit into the woods and gullies was allowed, and the Crusaders retired on Arsouf in good order and made camp. It was the greatest of all Crusading victories, and it was won by generalship, forethought and control.

RESULTS OF THE THIRD CRUSADE

Saladin still had an army, but it was too shaken to make another stand in the open. Nor could he trust his troops to make a determined defence of the remaining coastal fortresses. He dismantled and abandoned all save one, which quickly fell, and retired into the interior. Richard's victory at Arsouf recovered the coast for the Christians but its full benefits were never reaped. When in due course he moved from Jaffa towards Jerusalem, disputes between the different interests and nationalities in his force made progress impossible ; and he was obliged to come to terms with Saladin. The Treaty of 1192 left the coast in Frankish possession, and allowed pilgrims to visit Jerusalem, but all the interior remained in Muslim hands. Many tales are told of the personal respect and esteem which Richard and Saladin came to share, and the courtesies exchanged between them. Though enemies in war and religion, they recognised in each other the knightly qualities in which each excelled.

Richard returned to the West, to a new campaign in Normandy against his former fellow-Crusader Philip Augustus, and Saladin died in 1193. The Franks were never to have another leader like Richard, but some two generations were to pass before the Muslims produced another like Saladin. The Third Crusade saved Frankish Syria from utter wreck, and Saladin's early death gave its remnants a long respite.

VIII CRUSADER CASTLES IN SYRIA

It is no accident that some of the finest examples of mediaeval Western castles are found not in Europe but in Syria. Castle building began from the first foundation of the Crusading States, and it continued for over a century and a half. Its necessity was obvious : the Franks' hold on Syria was shaky, their frontiers long and open to attack, and their man-power small. Only by building the strongest possible fortresses at border fords and passes and the ports could the few hope to hold out against the many.

EARLY CASTLES

The first castles built in Syria were comparatively small and simple, employing the square keep of the type the Normans were then building in England. But from the first the Crusaders improved on Western designs by borrowing ideas from the Greeks and possibly also from the Saracens. The Norman square keep was solid, but not dangerous to an attacker. There was no way of providing a flank fire along its walls, and no way of covering their foot without leaning right over the battlements, while the entrance was small and high up and sorties were almost impossible. " If it could be defended by one soldier, it could be besieged by two."

The Greeks had inherited the old Roman skill in fortification, and in their long struggle with the Muslims had improved it by devices which allowed a much more active defence. From them the Crusaders adopted projecting towers to give flanking fire, and the carrying forward of the parapet on stone brackets to allow the foot of the wall to be protected without exposing the defenders. Elaborate ditches, often hewn with immense labour through solid rock, were dug to block the approaches, and the lower portion of the walls was often sloped outwards to increase the thickness against battering machines.

Before the collapse of the Kingdom of Jerusalem in 1187, most castles consisted of a keep and an outer ring of curtain wall with towers. Examples of this type still remain amongst those which fell finally to the Muslims at this time and were therefore never reconstructed. It was after this, when the position of the remaining Frankish States was increasingly dangerous and their lack of man-power more marked, that the finest and most elaborate examples were built.

SITES OF CASTLES

Amongst the first castles was a line of seven between Jaffa and Jerusalem, designed to protect the pilgrim route and to house garrisons to patrol the road. In 1118 these were put in the charge of the Templars, who were first organised for this particular purpose. They were all small places, and did not play any notable part in the general defence of the Kingdom.

The most important were the strongholds sited to protect the borders, often

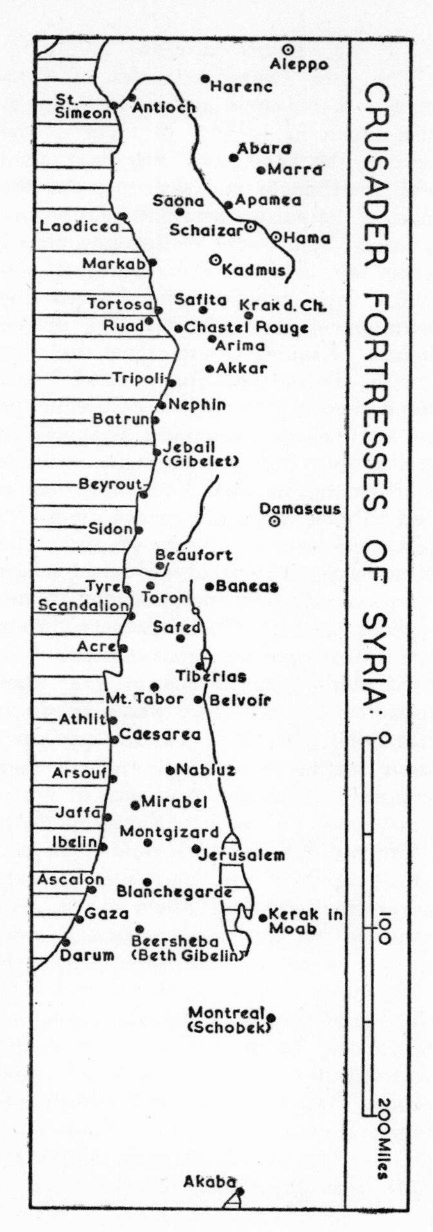

in remote and desolate places on mountain passes and river crossings, where distance from habitation has left some of them almost undisturbed and intact to the present day. From Saona south of Antioch to Beaufort near Sidon a single line was sufficient to hold the gaps through the otherwise impassable Lebanon Mountains, with the help of the two Assassin strongholds of Kadmus and Masiaf. But farther south, where natural defences were less strong, successive lines were needed. East of the Jordan the fortress of Baneas covered the fords of the upper river, and the line Kerak–Montreal–Akaba spanned the gap between the Dead Sea and the Akaba Gulf. West of the Upper Jordan the line Toron–Safed–Belvoir covered another dangerous front, and a network of castles blocked the routes into the Kingdom of the South.

CASTLES OF THE MILITARY ORDERS

These border castles, perched on rocky crags and far from the pleasures and comforts of town life, were not attractive places for the ordinary feudal knight to garrison. Nor, as they became more expensive to build and maintain, could the resources of king and barons easily bear the burden. It was here that the Military Orders stepped in to solve the problem. As men vowed to the life of a religious community, they found isolation an advantage rather than a drawback : and as warriors devoted to the Holy War, without estates of their own to worry about, they made ideal frontier garrisons. Their wealth in the West provided the funds necessary to build and equip these increasingly elaborate fortresses, while their organisation in Europe kept up a supply of new recruits to man them.

As organised bodies with an unbroken existence they avoided also one of the outstanding weaknesses of the feudal baronage in Syria—the effect of the baron's sudden death at an awkward moment and without an adult heir. The first castles had been built and held by barons, but before long they were glad to turn most of them over to the Hospitallers or Templars. By 1166 only three castles south of Beyrout remained in private hands. Not only did the Orders take over existing castles (and often rebuild them) but they built new ones. The Templars came to hold eighteen fortresses, including Tortosa, Safita, Arima, Beaufort, Safed, and Athlit : while the Hospitallers held, amongst others, Markab, Krak des Chevaliers, Baneas, Ibelin, Beersheba, and Belvoir. The castles were the keys of the Kingdom, and with them the Orders took over the main responsibility for its defence.

The third group were those protecting the seaport towns. These too had a most important part to play, for on them depended the sea-communications of the Crusading States with the West. Consequently, they were all built on the shore, and often on promontories which could be easily defended against land attack. Unlike the border castles, they were not isolated. They all lay close to the thriving trading cities in which the wealth and Frankish population of the States were concentrated, and which remained inhabited when Crusader rule was over. As a result, they have mostly been demolished for their materials ; and only in the interior can castles be seen today almost as the last knights left them.

LATER CASTLES

The later Crusader castles of Syria show a massiveness and an intricacy of plan much in advance of those of the time in the West, and they were sited with forethought and skill to make the most of natural features like hilltops and ravines. Some were deliberately placed where they could be seen, over great distances, from other strongholds, so that communications could be kept up by signals. Beaufort could signal direct to Baneas, Toron, and Sidon : and Toron could relay signals to the castles of the Jordan Valley. A similar arrangement existed between the fortresses on the southern border, and Kerak-in-Moab is said to have made fire-signals nightly to Jerusalem over a distance of fifty miles when besieged by Saladin in 1183. Where direct signals were not possible, carrier pigeons (whose use had been learned from the Arabs) were employed instead.

Saladin's great sweep in 1187 took many castles, but those whose garrisons had not been lost at Tiberias put up a stout resistance and only fell through famine after sieges of a year or more. Such were Belvoir, Kerak-in-Moab, Montreal, Safed, and Beaufort. Some, including Montreal and Kerak, were never recovered. Others when they returned to Christian possession were made still more formidable. A great earthquake in 1202 damaged nearly all the Syrian castles, and made rebuilding necessary. Fortresses built or reconstructed after 1190 are mostly of 'concentric' design, with two complete and separate lines of defence on all sides, except where attack was quite impossible from some directions.

Krak des Chevaliers

KRAK DES CHEVALIERS

One of the greatest, and now the best preserved, of these is Krak des Chevaliers on the mountain border of Tripoli. This great work, which defied twelve sieges, was built in its present form by the Hospitallers about 1205. It crowns the end of a commanding spur above the pass, and was designed for a garrison of some 2,000 men. The inner ward has its walls sloping outwards at the foot to the immense thickness of 80 feet on the side exposed to attack, and its massive towers completely dominate the outer ward which surrounds it. The entrance is cunningly contrived at a point which it was difficult for an enemy to reach, and leads from the outer to the inner gateway through a long narrow passage barred by successive gates. The walls of the outer ward are protected by a succession of projecting stone boxes, which allow their

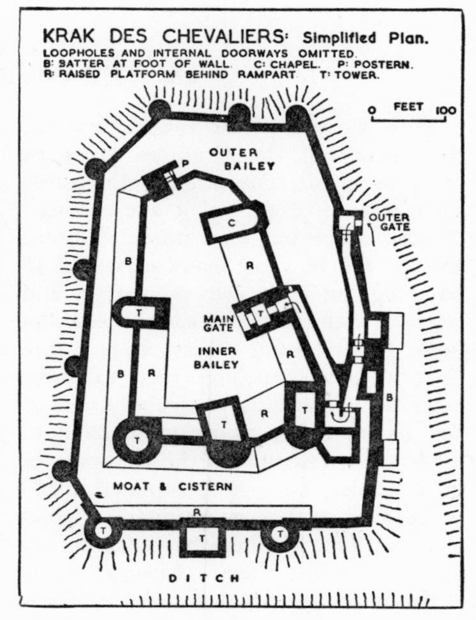

foot to be covered by concealed fire, and a ditch was hewn through the solid rock on the only side where the ground gave room for siege works. It fell at last in 1271, but only because it had but a tenth of the garrison it was designed for.

THE END OF THE CASTLES

The same reason explained the eventual fall of most of the Crusader castles which prolonged the Frankish foothold in Syria until the late thirteenth century. Famine was not, as in earlier times, a common cause of surrender, for places like Markab with storerooms sufficient for 1,000 men for five years could have fed their greatly reduced numbers almost indefinitely. As the Crusading enthusiasm waned in the West, new recruits became fewer and the confidence of those in Syria was undermined. No chance of ultimate victory remained, and a settled gloom seems to have fallen on those who were left. In the end they were too few to make full use of their magnificent fortifications and to prolong the defence by sorties, and castle after castle fell for lack of men or lack of hope. In a few cases mining by the besiegers brought about surrender, as at Markab in 1285 ; but even this could have been prevented by countermining if the defenders had been sufficiently numerous. The real reason for the final collapse of the Crusading castles lay not in any weakness in themselves but in the failure of the Crusading spirit in the West on which they relied for support. There were limits to the power of stones to make up for lack of men.

IX THE FOURTH CRUSADE

With the end of the twelfth century, the history of the Crusades takes an ominous turn. The original Crusading spirit was not dead, but it was waning : the call which had once united Western Europe fell now on many ears deaf to anything but their own advantage, and religious enthusiasm was sometimes a disguise for following private ends rather than a force impelling men to make sacrifices. This was particularly true of the Italian cities, whose naval strength made them essential to the transport of great armies, but whose commercial advantage lay rather in keeping on good terms with the Muslims than in encouraging war against them. Meanwhile, as Western Europe began to sort itself out into national States, kings found themselves too much concerned with the business of government and with conflicts with their neighbours to play a leading part in Crusades. There were exceptions, both amongst rulers and knights, but in general the great days of Crusading were over.

The peculiar history of the Fourth Crusade illustrates the change. It was launched by the great Pope Innocent III, with the ambitious object of ending the internal quarrels of Christendom, recovering the Holy Land, and uniting the Roman Catholic and Greek Orthodox Churches, so that in future there might be a common Christian front against the Turk. But though the Pope set it moving, he could not control it once it had started : and its results were the very opposite of his intentions.

VENICE INTERVENES

No kings came forward, and the response was mainly from the barons and knights of France and Flanders. These assembled at Venice in 1201 to find shipping for their passage to the East. The knights, whose outlook was nearest to that of earlier Crusaders, wanted to go direct to Palestine, while their leaders had a plan for attacking Egypt. Either scheme had much in its favour, for Egypt was then the centre of Muslim power in the Near East, and its conquest would have made the recovery of the Holy Land easy : but neither plan suited the Venetians. Venice had a treaty with the Sultan of Egypt, which gave her valuable trading privileges in Egyptian ports, while in Syria her interests did not stretch farther than the coastal towns where she was already established. War in either direction would interrupt trade and could only cause her losses, but the Doge was astute enough to see that the strength of the Crusade might be used to serve the purposes of Venice elsewhere. He did not refuse to take them to the East : instead he made them agree to a price which they could not pay, and so obliged them to accept the Venetian plan instead.

The first action of this remarkable Crusade was to attack the Christian city of Zara on the Adriatic, and hand it over to Venice. Its next was even more surprising. The Emperor Alexius III of Constantinople had recently deposed the incompetent Emperor Isaac, and Isaac's son appeared in the West in hopes of finding support to expel Alexius and restore his father. He offered a great sum of money, an army to help reconquer Syria, and a permanent cavalry force to defend it. The first offer aroused the greed of the barons, and the rest eased their consciences by allowing them to argue that, in turning aside against Alexius, they were still helping the cause of the Holy Land. The Venetians were delighted : they had a private quarrel with Alexius, who had favoured their rivals of Pisa at their expense, and they had great hopes of gain if they could establish themselves firmly in the Eastern Empire.

CAPTURE OF CONSTANTINOPLE

It was therefore decided to attack Constantinople. Pope Innocent was outraged and forbade it, but he was disregarded. Some knights too were disgusted, and left for Palestine, where they managed to recover Nazareth for a short while. But the main Crusading host arrived in June, 1203, to besiege the ancient Christian capital. Neglect of the Byzantine fleet allowed them to ignore the famous triple walls and attack from the sea ; and within a month they entered the city, restored Isaac, and called on him to make good his son's promises. Isaac could not. His own subjects rebelled against an Emperor proved incompetent and only restored by the force of foreign 'barbarians', and the Crusaders determined instead to have done with him and make themselves masters of his Empire.

In April, 1204, they seized the city again, pillaged it for three days with every form of violence, and then divided the spoils. A Frankish Empire was set

The Fourth Crusade attacks Constantinople

up, with vassal states on the Syrian model, and Venice received three-eighths of Constantinople and a great number of easily defended and commercially important coastal towns and islands. Pope Innocent's great design had resulted in the smashing of Christendom's chief eastern bulwark, and in a final breach between the Greeks and the West which made any future common stand against the Turk impossible.

PARTITION OF THE BYZANTINE EMPIRE

The Latin Empire of Constantinople did not by any means include all the Byzantine territories. The Greek Emperors re-established themselves at Nicaea, and Greek rulers continued in Epirus and Trebizond. Threatened by these, and by the hostile Bulgarians, the hold of the Franks on the lands of the Aegean was shaky from the first. As in Syria, there were too few of them and their interests were too divided, while the Greeks they ruled remained sullenly hostile. We are hardly surprised in the circumstances to find the 'Crusading' Emperor in 1209 making an alliance with the Turkish Sultan against his Greek fellow-Christians. The attempt to unite the Greek Orthodox Church with Rome by force was a dismal failure. Though a Venetian Patriarch said the Roman Mass in Santa Sophia, the Greek bishops fled to Nicaea and continued to encourage their flocks in resistance.

The Latin Empire of Constantinople had a short and stormy history, and in 1261 the Greek Emperor of Nicaea ended it by retaking the capital. But the Greeks did not recover all that had been lost in 1204. Frankish Dukes of Athens and

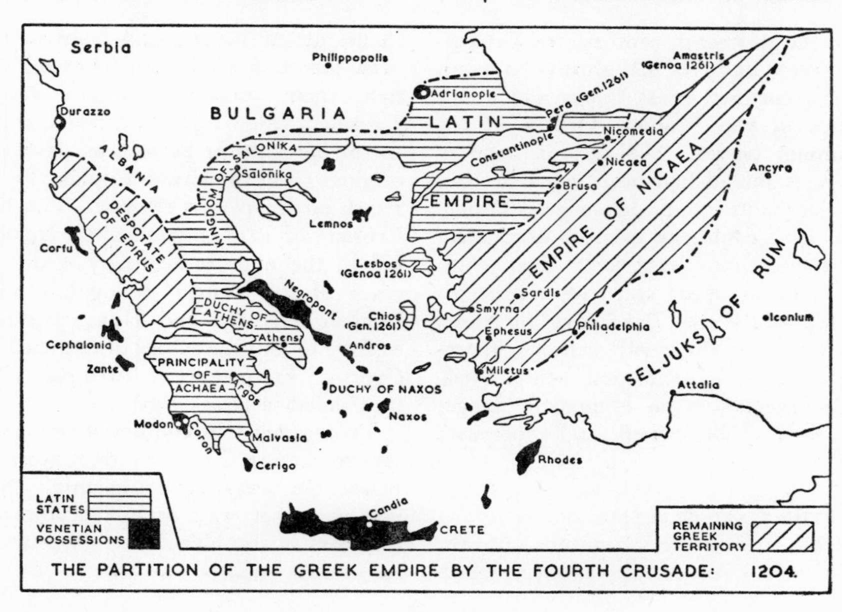

THE PARTITION OF THE GREEK EMPIRE BY THE FOURTH CRUSADE: 1204.

Princes of Achaea continued for some time longer, and the islands and some of the ports remained in Venetian hands till after the Greek Empire finally vanished. Other islands had to be handed to Genoa, as the price of her help against Venice. Though the Greeks held Constantinople for nearly two centuries more, the damage was beyond repair. The gains they had made as a result of the First Crusade were more than cancelled by the ruin caused by the Fourth, and they were left powerless against the coming onrush of the Ottoman Turks. The remaining Crusading States in Syria suffered too, for men and resources which might have prolonged their existence were diverted to prop up the tottering Latin rulers of Constantinople.

In the West, also, the Fourth Crusade had a most unfortunate result, for it debased the whole meaning of the word Crusade and the spirit behind it. From then onwards 'Crusades' could be launched against Christians as well as against the Infidel, and any war which had the Pope's approval might be so termed. Such were the 'Crusade' of 1208 against the Albigensian heretics of Southern France, and the war which followed John of England's defiance of the Pope.

But Crusaders of the original breed were not yet extinct, and some genuine Crusades were yet to come.

X THE LAST CRUSADES, AND THE END OF FRANKISH SYRIA

In the thirteenth century, the Crusading States in Syria had shrunk to a few heavily fortified coast towns and a few castles of the Military Orders in the mountain passes. All serious hope of conquest inland had been given up, but the remnants were defensively strong. The ports could not even be blockaded, for the Italian fleets kept their communications open and the Christians dominated the sea. The Crusading efforts of the earlier thirteenth century, therefore, are less concerned with Syria, where there was no immediate danger and little to be gained, and more with Egypt.

THE FIRST EGYPTIAN CRUSADE

After the pathetic episode of the Children's Crusade in 1212 (in which thousands of French and German children marched off in the touching hope that their innocence would recover Jerusalem where force had failed, only to die of hardship or be sold as slaves) the original Fourth Crusade plan for an attack on Egypt was revived. The Fifth Crusade of 1217, organised by Innocent III in the hope of wiping out the disgrace of the Fourth, brought a mixed English, German and Hungarian force to Acre to join the Kings of Armenia and Cyprus. From there in 1218 part of the host sailed to attack Egypt.

To conquer that country it was necessary to capture Cairo, and there were two reasonable ways of doing this : by a landing either west or east of the river branches of the Nile Delta. Westwards, Alexandria offered a base ; but this

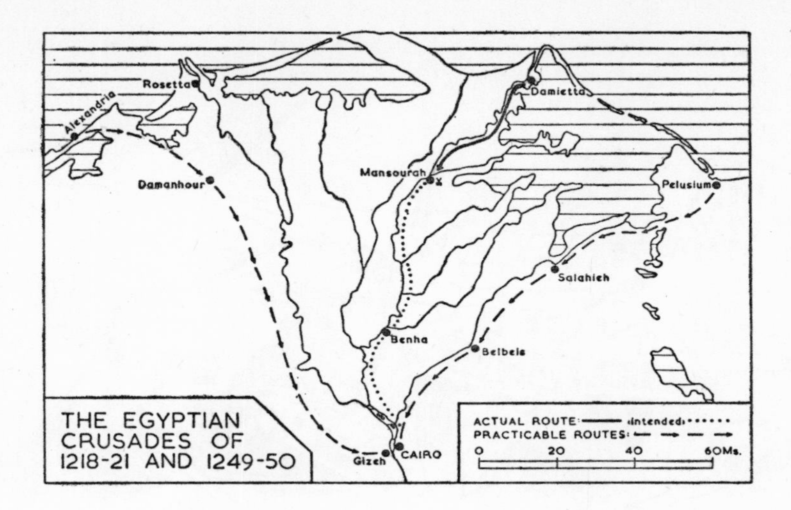

route involved a long desert march and would bring an army opposite Cairo on the wrong side of the river. Eastwards, it was possible to march straight to the city; but there was no good harbour for the ships. The Crusaders of 1218, like their successors of 1249, chose neither route, but elected instead to take Damietta as a base and advance through the Delta across the successive branches of the Nile. This was disastrous, for at every crossing the defenders had a first-class obstacle, and at need they could cut the dikes and flood the low-lying country.

The expedition led by John of Brienne spent eight months besieging Damietta, and then was brought to a full stop by the line of the Ashmoum Canal. They could not break across it, and their communications with their base were cut by flooding. They only saved themselves by agreeing to hand back Damietta and depart (1221). A thoroughly bad plan of campaign had put them in a hopeless position where they could achieve nothing and could not even come to grips with their enemy.

ST. LOUIS IN EGYPT

Yet precisely the same plan was followed, with even worse results, by St. Louis of France in the Seventh Crusade of 1249. He captured Damietta without difficulty, but then wasted six months before he advanced to the Ashmoum Canal. Every attempt to bridge it by a causeway was met by heavy fire and by cutting back the bank on the other side, and for two months the armies lay facing each other across the barrier. When advance seemed hopeless a ford usable by cavalry was discovered; and a plan was made to get the horsemen across, seize the Egyptian engines which prevented work on the causeway, and cover the bank until the infantry could close the gap and cross. It was a reasonable scheme, and in the circumstances

The Charge at Mansourah

the only possible one, and it might have succeeded but for a typical piece of indiscipline.

The leader of the cavalry vanguard ignored his orders to wait for the rest, and charged straight into the Egyptian camp. The surprise was complete, and he reached the bank opposite the causeway without difficulty. Had he halted there and held it while the infantry got to work and the rest of the cavalry came up in support, the foot might have been brought into battle while the Muslims were still disorganised. Instead, he went off on a mad charge into the near by town of Mansourah and his whole force was cut to pieces. St. Louis with the rest fought through to the place, and eventually got his infantry over, but only after half his cavalry had been lost. It was a drawn battle, and in these circumstances a draw was a defeat. He could advance no farther, but was loath to retire till disease and famine compelled him. As he retreated a running fight cut his army to pieces, and he himself was captured with the remnants. The faults of so many Crusading armies—ignorance of geography, refusal to learn from previous disasters, and neglect of orders—had combined to ruin an expedition which might have been resoundingly successful.

FREDERICK II

Meanwhile, through most of the first half of the thirteenth century, affairs in Syria had been comparatively peaceful. The Muslims were once more divided, and it was even possible for two brief moments to recover Jerusalem. The first occasion resulted from the Sixth Crusade of Frederick II of Germany in 1228.

Frederick II

Frederick II, known as ' Stupor Mundi ' —' the wonder of the world ', was an amazing character for a mediaeval monarch. Of great culture and intelligence, but of little faith, he had delighted from his earliest days in the friendship of Muslim scholars in his realm of Sicily. Tolerant to the point of having apparently no religious convictions at all, he soon fell foul of the Pope and was excommunicated. Under the ban of the Church, he set out on Crusade !

The clergy of Palestine refused to have anything to do with him, or the Military Orders to serve under his banner : yet he recovered Jerusalem without fighting. He had already exchanged friendly embassies with the Sultan El Kamil, and came to an agreement with him for a ten-year truce and the return to Christian

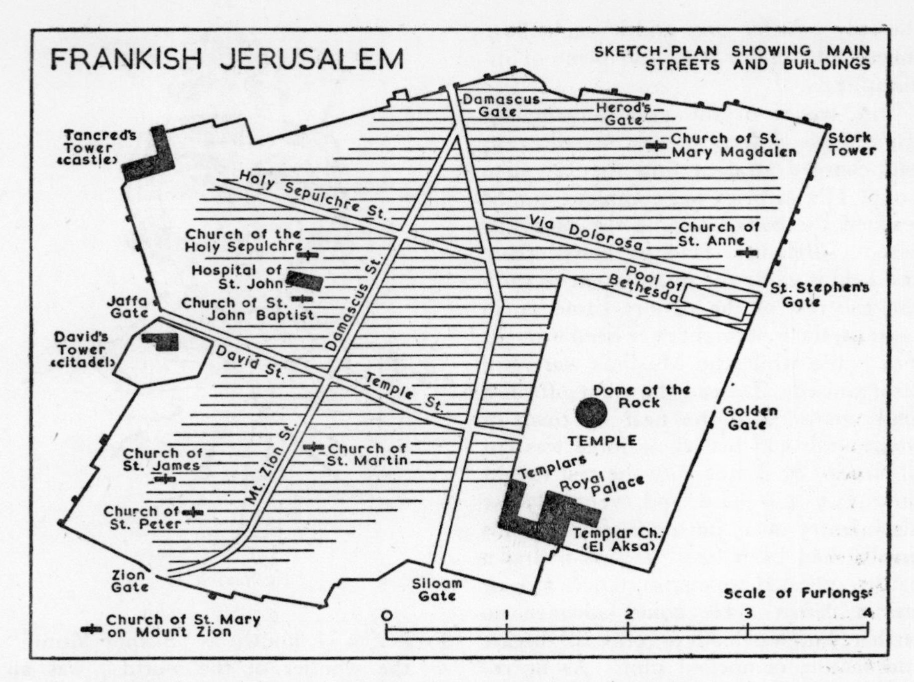

hands of Jaffa, Bethlehem, Nazareth, Sidon, Toron, Montfort, and most of Jerusalem except for the Temple and the Muslim Holy Places in the city (1229). In the Church of the Holy Sepulchre he crowned himself King of Jerusalem (since no clergy would do it for him) and with his usual impartiality paid a respectful visit to the Muslim Mosque of Omar.

This sort of thing was beyond the comprehension of the Syrian Franks, let alone the Westerners ; and the Templars were bitter at his effortless success where they had failed and at his leaving their great church in the Temple in Muslim hands. The Pope rewarded him with an interdict on his new kingdom, and he returned to the West to find himself once more excommunicated and his lands invaded by Papal forces.

Though he remained King of Jerusalem till his death in 1250, he never visited Palestine again and the city was soon lost. His absence left free scope for conflicts and disorders to develop in the remaining Frankish possessions, and only the temporary divisions of their Muslim neighbours preserved them. One such allowed the Christians to recover Jerusalem again in 1244, by alliance with one Muslim faction against another, but this was only momentary. Within a few months the other side called in the Charismians, an Asian horde pushed into Mesopotamia by the conquests of the famous Jenghiz Khan, and these took

The Mosque of Omar, Jerusalem

(or, Dome of the Rock, built in the seventh century on the site of the Temple at Jerusalem to protect the rock from which Mohammed is said to have ascended to heaven)

and sacked Jerusalem. It was never again to be in Christian hands till British forces entered in 1917. An ill-judged battle against the same foe at Gaza in the same year proved disastrous. Of 300 Templars present only four survived, and both Grand Masters were captured. After this the final collapse was only a matter of time.

DIVISIONS AND DECLINE IN SYRIA

In these last days the jealousies which had always blighted the Frankish cause in Syria showed at their worst. In 1249 the Pisans and Genoese were at open war in Acre, and in 1256 the Genoese and Venetians opened a struggle, in which others took sides, which lasted four years. The Templars and Hospitallers also reached the point of fighting, and no supreme authority remained to hold the Franks together. There were too many rival interests, each out for their own ends, to make common cause against the final Muslim assault.

In 1260 the Mongols invaded Syria, as part of the great wave of conquest which submerged China, most of Asia, and Eastern Europe. They took Aleppo, Hama, and Damascus, but their advance was then checked. The Sultan, after appealing vainly to the Franks for help, met them and turned them back. Having done so, he turned upon the Franks. In 1265 Arsouf and Caesarea fell, in the following year Safed, and in 1268 Jaffa and the great city of Antioch. The loss of Antioch evoked what was

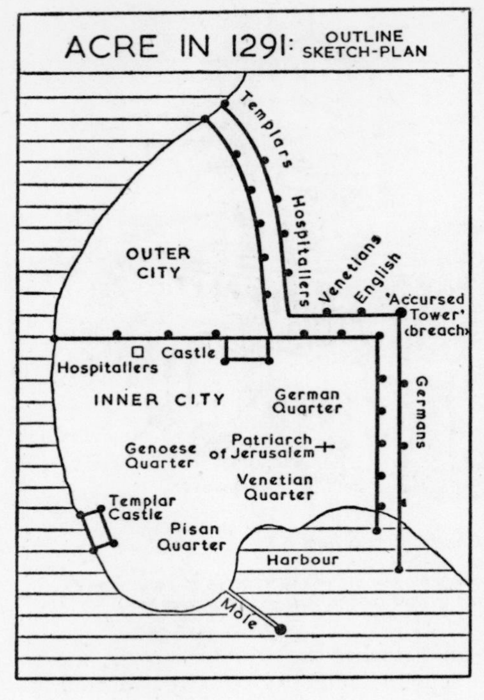

practically the last Crusade, the expedition of 1270 by St. Louis of France and Prince Edward (later Edward I) of England. St. Louis took his forces to Tunis, because of an unfounded rumour that the local Bey might turn Christian : he achieved nothing, and died there. Edward reached Acre, too late to save the great Krak des Chevaliers which fell in 1271, and could do no more than arrange a ten-year truce. The remnants of Tripoli were now paying tribute to Sultan Bibars, and after the truce expired his successors carried on the war. The huge fortress of Markab fell in 1285, and the city of Tripoli in 1289.

As place after place was taken, those Franks who escaped death or slavery took refuge in Acre. Towards the end this final stronghold became crowded with refugees, adding to the confusion which already prevailed. Within its wall were seventeen distinct groups from Western trading towns and nations, all at bitter feud, along with the Templars and Hospitallers at daggers drawn. No sense of common cause remained, and no party was ready to help another or to defend anything outside its own quarter. When the assault came in 1291 it was a matter of each for himself : the only stout defence was that of the Templars, who fought till their castle was undermined and brought down over their heads. The victorious Muslims massacred their captives and blocked the port with the wreck of the fortifications, and Christian Syria came to a final and bloody end. The remaining formidable strongholds of Tortosa, Athlit, Beyrout, and Sidon were abandoned without a fight, and only the island castle of Ruad off Tortosa was held till 1303. The Venetians, true to type, lost no time in making a trading treaty with the victors.

So ended the first European experiment in overseas colonisation, and with it, for all practical purposes, the history of the Crusades. A few expeditions of adventurers went in the fourteenth century to help Greeks and Hungarians against the Turk, but they achieved little, It was not their efforts but the attacks of the Mongol Timurlane which delayed the Ottoman conquest of Constantinople and the Balkans. Future fighting in the East between Christian and Muslim was to be for the defence of national inde-

The Fall of Acre

pendence, or possessions and trading profits, rather than for religion.

But while in the Eastern Mediterranean Christendom was forced back on the defensive by the growing pressure of the Turks, in the far West a lengthy but victorious war of liberation had freed Portugal and nearly all Spain. This was a national war, but in some ways it also belongs to the story of the Crusades.

XI THE RECONQUEST OF SPAIN AND PORTUGAL

The first rush of Muslim conquest in the early eighth century carried the banners of Islam to the line of the Pyrenees and at the eastern end beyond them into France. All Christian Spain was submerged, save only a narrow strip along the northern coast protected by the mountain range of the Asturias. Yet from the mountain glens, and the foothills of the Pyrenees recovered by Charlemagne at the end of the century, was to come the counter-attack which gradually pushed back Islam across the Straits of Gibraltar.

ARAB SPAIN

For many years there was little sign of this. The hardy mountaineers of the North, with their small separate kingdoms of Leon, Castile, Aragon, and Navarre, could not compete with the wealth and power of the Emirate of Cordoba. Under tolerant Arab rule there grew a civilisation which far outshone that of its poverty-stricken Christian neighbours, and which made Spain a land of cities, universities, and craftsmen while Western Europe was sunk in the Dark Ages. The Arabs taught the science and philosophy of Ancient Greece at a time when it was unknown in the West, and used the architects and artists of Byzantium to create towns whose mosques, libraries, and public baths were the wonder of Christian visitors. Under Arab rule the Christian population mostly lived undisturbed, and were even allowed to serve as soldiers and officials.

Throughout the ninth and tenth centuries there was little change ; but in the early eleventh century the same influences which encouraged the eastern Crusades began to work in the Peninsula. In 1031 the Emirate of Cordoba broke up into rival petty states, and a Christian counter-attack became possible, while soon afterwards the stirrings of revival which produced the First Crusade made themselves felt in Spain. The recapture of Toledo by the King of Castile in 1085, with the help of knights from France, Germany, and Italy, began the Reconquest which was to continue for three centuries.

SPANISH WARFARE

Spain, " where large armies starve and small ones get beaten," is well known as a difficult country for warfare. Its mountain ranges running parallel from west to east, its bad roads, and its great areas of infertile plateau, make organised campaigns difficult. The forces of the Spanish kingdoms, like Crusading hosts in the East, had little organisation in any case, and it was exceptional for two or more kings to act together against the

Spanish-Muslim Architecture
Gateway to the Court of the Maidens, Alcazar of Seville

common foe. Fighting was more a matter of raids than of pitched battles, and a form of tactics was developed here which owed much to Muslim models.

Mobility was essential over the great distances involved, and the favourite Spanish type of soldier came to be the fast and light-armed horseman with javelins. His duty was to raid and harass, like the Turkish horse-archer, and in battle to disorder an enemy line sufficiently to make way for the heavy charge of the knights. In Spain, as in Syria, besides the feudal baronage there developed the Military Orders, half monk and half warrior. The four great Orders of Calatrava, Alcantara, Evora, and Santiago formed the shock troops in battle and the mainstay of the defence. Infantry were not used much by either side, for the distances and difficulties of the country made them only a drag on mounted forces.

As in Syria, too, castles and walled towns played a great part. Castile took its name from the border fortresses built as refuges and protection from Muslim raids, and the growth of fortified towns was encouraged by the dangers of living exposed to sudden forays in the open

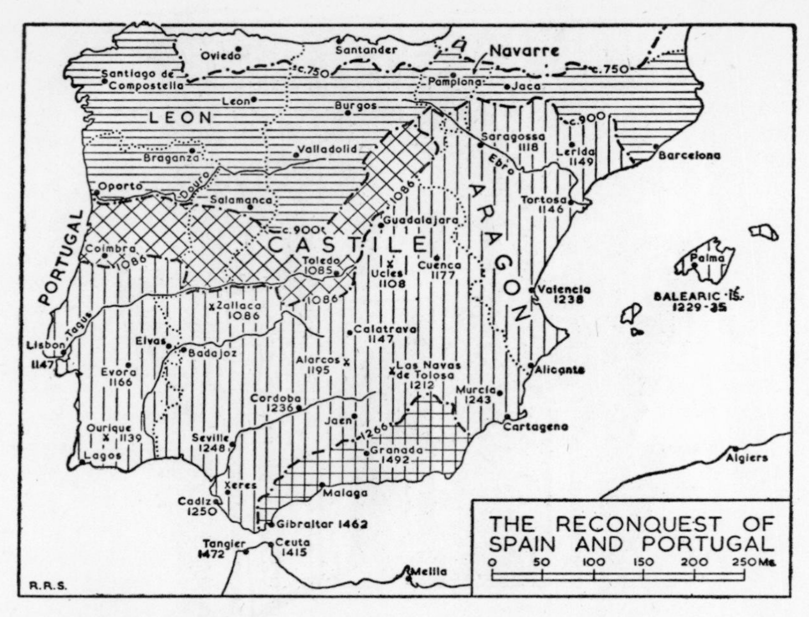

country. One result of this was the neglect of agriculture which continued in Spain even after the wars were over.

THE RECONQUEST

The capture of Toledo, which began the Reconquest, ended the greatest period of tolerant Arab civilisation. Its immediate result was the calling in of fanatical Berbers from North Africa—the Almoravides—who quickly made themselves masters of Muslim Spain and temporarily checked the Christian advance. In their nature, and in time, they correspond closely to the Turks in the East. These newcomers lacked Arab tolerance, and many Christian and Jewish refugees took shelter within the Christian kingdoms. From the scholars, translators, and craftsmen among them the West gained much of Arab learning and civilisation, and also by this surprising route recovered some of the lost thought and science of Ancient Greece.

One by-product of the otherwise futile Second Crusade was the capture of Lisbon in 1147 by English and German Crusaders on their way to Syria. This helped to ensure that Portugal, hitherto a mere county round Oporto, should become a Kingdom and in due course separate itself from the rest of Spain.

The Muslim recovery in Syria under Saladin was paralleled, at much the same time, by a new migration of fanatical Muslims into Spain. The Almohades, who displaced the Almoravides, rolled back the Christian advance once more at Alarcos in 1195. The struggle for Spain was in the balance, and much depended on which side showed the greatest unity. Fortunately for the Christian cause, the efforts of Pope Innocent III to persuade the various kings to act together bore fruit in the alliance of Aragon, Castile, and Navarre which won the great victory of Las Navas de Tolosa in 1212. This tipped the scale, and during the next fifty-four years a succession of victories by Castile and Aragon drove the Moors into the mountains of Granada. In this process these two kingdoms emerged as the leading powers of Spain. Castile finally absorbed Leon, and Aragon turned its attention overseas to the Balearic Islands and to Sicily. Navarre, cut off from expansion by the conquests of its neighbours, remained the tiny mountain state it had always been : and Portugal turned its back on the others and looked towards the Atlantic.

EFFECTS OF THE WAR OF RECONQUEST

After 1266—when the final extinction of the Frankish holdings in Syria was beginning—the struggle in Spain ceased and was not renewed for another two centuries. But much of the future character of Spain had already been decided. The long years of combined Crusade and War of Liberation had given Spain the strongly Catholic outlook which she has retained ever since, and had made the Church a very powerful element in her national life. One result of this was eventually the expulsion of Jews and Muslims from her soil, which did so much damage by removing men of skill and ability from her economic life.

The ravages and uncertainty of the centuries of war had left much of her soil a desert, from which it has never fully recovered. Spain emerged, and remained, poor but proud. The aristocracy of knights and barons which had led the Reconquest remained firmly established, alongside the Church, and there was never sufficient prosperity to produce a healthy growth of townsmen to challenge their supremacy. Even in the days of her later greatness, Spain preferred to control the gold and silver of America rather than to develop her own internal resources.

The eventual marriage of Ferdinand, who became King of Aragon in 1479, with Isabella, who succeeded to Castile in 1474, brought about the long-delayed assault on Granada with their united forces. In 1492 the last Emir surrendered his stronghold and rode into exile, and after nearly 800 hundred years the banner of the Crescent vanished from the soil of Spain.

But the Muslim occupation, unlike that of the Franks in Syria, had been too lengthy and too penetrating for its results to vanish without trace. Many of the place-names of Spain today are Arabic, and the Spanish language contains great numbers of Arab words. Music and architecture, especially in the south, owe much to Arab influence. As in Syria, there had been long periods of peace and friendly intercourse between the two civilisations, and the more advanced of the two was bound to make its impression. Had the remnants of the Moorish population—the Moriscos—not been expelled after the Reconquest at the bidding of the Church, the lasting influence would have been much greater. It is a curious thought that the 'Olé' of a Spanish singer is in origin an invocation of Allah.

The Surrender of Granada

XII THE EFFECTS OF THE CRUSADES

When we come to examine the results of the Crusades, we have at once to distinguish between their direct achievement and their indirect influence. The latter was by far the most important, but the former was by no means as short-lived as may at first appear. The fall of Acre in 1291 ended Christian rule on the mainland of Asia, but not in the East Mediterranean Islands. Cyprus provided a refuge for the knights of Syria, and remained till 1488 an independent Christian kingdom. It then passed into the hands of Venice, but still defied the Turk till 1571. Rhodes, captured by the Hospitallers in 1309, was defended by them till 1522, and the Venetians and Genoese held on to the Aegean Islands they had taken from the Greeks into the fifteenth and sixteenth centuries. Crete, indeed, was not lost till 1669.

All these Christian outposts, relics of the Crusades, helped to absorb the energies of Islam and delay the Ottoman onrush until Europe was ready to meet it, while in Spain the Reconquest finally decided that the Peninsula was to be a Christian and not a Muslim country. So deeply were the Spanish and Portuguese imbued with the Crusading spirit and tradition that their great overseas explorations and conquests of the fifteenth and sixteenth centuries were in a sense a continuation of the Crusade. This was particularly true of the Portuguese, who aimed to defeat the Turkish drive into Eastern Europe by striking at the centres of Muslim trade and wealth in the Indian Ocean. The great Albuquerque even planned to capture Mecca via the Red Sea, and compel the Muslims to restore Jerusalem in exchange ! In their original objects, however, the Crusades undoubtedly failed : only for a short time were the Holy Places brought under Christian rule, and the Eastern Empire was in the long run far more harmed than helped in its struggle with the Turk.

EFFECTS OF EASTERN CONTACTS

It is to the indirect results of the Crusades that we must look for their greatest effect on the history of Europe, and here again we must distinguish between the results of contact with the East on the one hand and the internal changes in the West to which the Crusades contributed. Contact with the East had already existed on a small scale before the Crusades began, and their effect was greatly to increase this rather than to begin it. Eastern products had not been unknown before 1095, but the trade which developed after the conquest of Syria made them much more common. Amongst the new crops introduced into Europe were rice, lemons, melons, and apricots. A large range of new cloths appeared to supplement the wool and linen of the West—cottons, muslins from Mosul, damasks from Damascus, sarsenets (' Saracen cloth ') and samite from Byzantium. Rugs, carpets, and tapestries found their way from the looms of

Syria, Persia, and Samarkand to the halls and castles of the West, and Eastern spices helped to make its diet palatable and to offer an alternative to salt for preserving meat through the winter. Glass mirrors, and works of art and craftsmanship in pottery, glass, precious metals, and enamels, all added to the amenities of the wealthy home.

TOWNS AND TRADE

Most of these goods, of course, were expensive luxuries beyond the reach of any but the well-to-do, but the trade in them, and the demand for cash to buy them, affected the lives of many humbler folk. Trade and town life had already been reviving in the West before the Crusades, and doubtless trade with the East would have developed if they had never taken place ; but the establishment of the Italian traders in Syria made this development far more rapid. Nobles and kings wanted money, for purchases or Crusading expenses, and to get it they sold privileges to towns or allowed their tenants to pay cash instead of their labour service.

The effect on the development of towns and commerce was naturally most marked in Italy. Venice and Genoa emerged as a result of the Crusades as powerful trading republics with overseas possessions, controlling a regular system of shipping in the Eastern Mediterranean for the transport of goods and pilgrims. They, with Pisa and Siena, early developed banking systems with Syrian branches, by which money could be transferred by credit note to or from the East or borrowed to finance trade. The Templars also had a flourishing banking business in Syria, with a special department for Muslim clients ; and the Venetians even struck a special gold coinage, with Arabic inscriptions from the Koran, for the Syrian trade. As the main importer of Eastern goods, Venice became the starting point of the great overland trade route across the Brenner Pass and down the Rhine to Flanders and North Germany, along or near which were concentrated so many of the important mediaeval towns.

KNOWLEDGE

Europe's knowledge of other lands and peoples was greatly widened by these Eastern contacts : but little of Arab science and scholarship seems to have come from Syria. The Franks there were either merchants or an army of occupation, while no great centres of Muslim learning were within reach. The Westerners adopted much of the daily life of the East, but saw and understood little of its higher civilisation. It was rather via Spain and Sicily that the West learnt Arab mathematics, science, medicine, and philosophy. Not only was Islamic culture much more brilliant in those countries, but it existed there alongside a large and balanced Christian population including scholars as well as warriors and traders. The introduction of Arabic numerals to the West may, however, be a result of Syrian commerce.

The Crusades opened new contacts with Constantinople as well as with Islam. For centuries since the fall of the West Roman Empire the civilisation of Byzantium, and the Greek language, had been almost unknown in the West. But from the time of the First Crusade con-

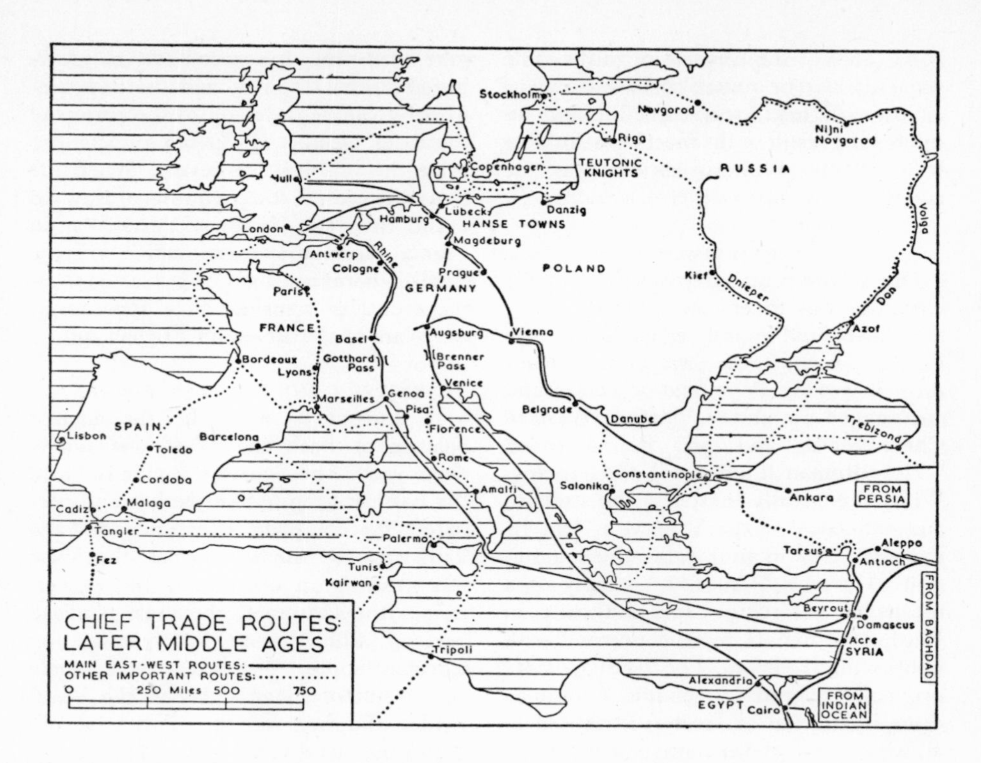

tact became much more frequent, and the Fourth actually established the Franks in the centre of the Empire. The Frankish conquerors of 1204 were not noticeably more cultivated than their Syrian counterparts : but their conquest opened direct access to Greek manuscripts, and encouraged the study of the Greek language, while the later advance of the Turks (helped by the Fourth Crusade) drove many Greek scholars to take refuge in the West in the fourteenth and fifteenth centuries. Ancient Greek learning, hitherto known only in part through translations from the Arabic, could now be reached at the source.

MILITARY EFFECTS

In military matters, too, the Crusades had their influence, though perhaps less than might be expected. The great Crusader castles of Syria, themselves partly the result of ideas borrowed from Arabs and Byzantines, became models for new building in the West ; and the siege-craft and engines of the Saracens were adopted in Western warfare. In tactics, however, the effect was small. The combination of crossbowmen with cavalry which proved so formidable in the Holy Land was little used at home, and the armoured knight continued to rule the battles of the West until the appearance of the English longbow. The use of padded or quilted coats, worn alone or beneath mail, was copied ; and an interesting result of the meeting of knights from all the Western nations was the adoption of uniform rules of heraldry.

THE PAPACY

One of the great internal effects of the Crusades was to enhance, for the time, the power and moral leadership of the Popes. In the great days of the movement it was the Pope who organised and encouraged the united efforts of Western Christendom, and not the so-called " Holy Roman Emperors " of Germany. While this greatly increased the strength and influence of the Papacy, it had its dangers ; for in time came the temptation to preach ' Crusades ' simply as a means of enforcing Papal authority in Europe in matters more concerned with politics than religion. The ' Indulgences ' originally offered to genuine Crusaders came in time to be freely distributed to all who, for whatever motive, assisted the political ends of the Pope, and this became one of the abuses which so damaged the Church in the later Middle Ages. Taxes raised by the Pope on the incomes of the clergy for purposes of Crusade continued to be collected as ordinary Papal revenue, and kings similarly made Crusades an excuse for taxation. The ' Saladin Tithe ' raised by Henry II in 1188 to finance the Third Crusade was made an excuse for a regular tax on income and movable property.

One beneficial effect was the draining off from the West of many warlike characters who would otherwise have found an outlet for their energies at home. This may have been one reason for the growing authority of kings, and the improvement in public order up to the period of the Black Death. It was not sufficient to solve the problem, however. When the Crusades ceased, the conquests of Edward I and then the Hundred Years War in France kept the more active of the English baronage busy : but as soon as these outlets vanished they fought out the Wars of the Roses on English soil.

EASTERN AND WESTERN EUROPE

In Europe as a whole, the ancient balance of East and West was finally destroyed. The Fourth Crusade reduced the Eastern Empire to a shadow and prepared its complete overthrow by the Turk, just at the time when the West was growing in civilisation and power. Before the Crusades, the most civilised part of Christendom had centred on Constantinople : afterwards, and largely as a result of them, it lay in the West. Under the heel of the Turk the old Byzantine lands fell back into semi-barbarism, while the vigorous new life and culture of France and its neighbours took its place as the fount of Christian and European civilisation.

DAILY LIFE

Europe of the fourteenth century was very different from that of the eleventh Even in the countryside, which had changed least, much land had been cleared and cultivation had extended, though the life of the peasant was probably little less monotonous and toilsome. Amongst the townsmen, and the knightly class, and the clergy and scholars, great developments had occurred. Towns in

general were much larger and more numerous, and their inhabitants more comfortable, prosperous, and independent. Trade, and the use of money, had greatly increased, and the households of the wealthy bore no comparison with the bare, dark, draughty halls of the Normans. Architecture, arts, and craftsmanship had made great progress : their products were not only better but much more plentiful. Universities were appearing where they had never been known before, and the horizons of men's minds had greatly widened.

Not all this was the result of the Crusades. Much of it would no doubt have happened if they had never taken place, for the beginnings of these developments were already visible before 1095. But in the extent and the rapidity of the process they played a notable part. Nor was their contribution only one of material progress. They gave Western Christendom an idea of common interest and purpose which has never been completely lost, and an ideal of unselfish service in a good cause to which we still apply the word ' Crusade '.

EXPLANATORY NOTES

Albuquerque : Founder of the Portuguese Empire in the Indian Ocean, died 1515. Captured Goa, Malacca, and Ormuz from the Muslims, but failed to take Aden. Bitterly anti-Muslim. like most Portuguese of his time.

Armenians : Originally a people living in the mountainous borderland between what is now Russia and Turkey, where some remain today. As a result of the Seljuk invasions many migrated to Cilicia or Lesser Armenia on the Mediterranean coast opposite Cyprus, shortly before the First Crusade. Here they maintained themselves in alliance with the Syrian Franks and the Kings of Cyprus till their last fortress fell to the Turks in 1375. The Turks deprived them of their nobility and organisation, and they became a scattered people dependent mainly on commerce.

Barbary Pirates : Corsairs of the North African coast from Tangier to Tunis, whose galleys captured Christian ships and enslaved their crews and passengers for centuries. The jealousies of European States prevented any united action against them, and their activities were not finally quelled till the French conquest of North Africa in the nineteenth century.

Bosphorus : The straits between Constantinople and Asia Minor, forming the eastern part of the passage from the Mediterranean to the Black Sea via the Dardanelles and the Sea of Marmora.

Byzantium : Ancient name of the city which was made eastern capital of the Roman Empire and renamed by Constantine in A.D. 330. The East Roman Empire which survived the barbarian invasions of the fifth century is commonly called ' Byzantine '.

Chivalry : Originally meaning ' cavalry ', and hence the rules of knightly honour and behaviour evolved in the Crusading period as a code of ' professional conduct ' for the governing warrior-class. In general, chivalry aimed to match the courage of the warrior with the courtesy and honourable dealing of the ' gentle knight ', and to limit the abuse of force against those unable to defend themselves. Also by implication the outward forms of knighthood, such as the tournament and heraldry.

Crescent : The crescent-moon symbol of Islam, the Muslim counterpart of the Cross. Hence the Turkish ' Red Crescent ' as part of the International Red Cross organisation.

Eastern Empire—see Byzantium.

Excommunication : Spiritual outlawry : the solemn exclusion of an individual from the sacraments and services of the Church, involving damnation if he died without previously being reconciled. It included a similar threat against any who associated with or helped the excommunicated person.

Franks : Originally the barbarian invaders who conquered, and gave their name to, France. Used at the Crusading period to include all Westerners, and still used in that sense by Muslims (' Feringhi '). The ' Lingua Franca ' of the time was a compound of French and Italian used as the language of commerce all over the Mediterranean.

Heraldry : Originating with the use of distinguishing signs on shields or garments to show the identity of an armoured knight in battle. Developing during and after the Crusading period into an elaborate and recognised system, controlled by the Royal Heralds.

Holy Roman Empire : First established in A.D 800 by the Papacy to give Christendom a Temporal Head independent of the Byzantine Emperor. Charlemagne, the first Emperor, ruled nearly all Western Christendom except the British Isles : but later, while the extent of Christendom grew, the Imperial authority became restricted to Germany and North Italy and even there became increasingly feeble. Mediaeval theory regarded the Pope as the spiritual and the Emperor as the temporal heads of a united Christendom ; but in practice it proved impossible to keep their spheres of authority separate, and the struggle which followed ended in the triumph of the Papacy and the practical eclipse of the Empire.

Indulgences : Strictly, the remission of punishment for sin granted to one who has truly repented ; but tending in the later Middle Ages to be granted in return for a money contribution for Church purposes.

Interdict : A papal decree closing churches and partially suspending the sacraments of the Church over a considerable area (e.g., throughout England during the reign of John). Used mainly as a means of putting pressure on rulers.

Islam : The Muslim religion (see pages 2–3) and in a general sense the lands where that religion prevailed : compare ' Christendom.'

Jenghiz Khan—see Mongols.

Koran : The Muslim Sacred Book, containing the revelations of the Prophet Mohammed and the bases of Muslim law.

Latins : Used as an alternative for ' Franks ', to distinguish Westerners of the Roman or Latin Church from Greeks.

Law Merchant : A body of commercial law and practice, much of it dating back to Roman times, designed to meet the special needs and problems of traders which were mostly ignored by feudal or customary law. Administered by special tribunals which could give speedy judgment without the delays of the ordinary courts (e.g., the ' Pie Powder ' courts of the great fairs).

Magyars : Hungarians : a people of Asian origin, from the area of the Urals. They settled in the present Hungary about A.D. 896, but continued to invade neighbouring countries until their great defeat near Augsburg in 995. They were later organised as a State by St. Stephen, who in A.D. 1000 adopted Roman Christianity and accepted the Hungarian Crown from the Pope.

Mecca : An Arabian religious centre long before Islam, containing the ancient Kaaba or cubic temple from which Mohammed displaced the earlier idols. It remained the chief centre of pilgrimage after the change of religion, as the Jewish holy city of Jerusalem did for the Christians.

Mongols : Nomad horsemen of the Asian steppes, who under Jenghiz Khan (died 1227) and his successors built up a vast but transitory empire. For a time they clung to their own primitive religion, and there was some hope in the West that they might be converted to Christianity and thereby challenge Islam in Asia. But missionary efforts, though made, were quite inadequate ; and by the end of the thirteenth century most of them accepted Islam. It was during the reign of Kublai Khan, towards the end of the century, that Marco Polo made his famous travels in Asia.

Moors : Used loosely by Westerners for Muslims in general (c.f. Feringhi for Christians) but more strictly applied to those of Spain and North Africa.

Mosque of Omar (or 'Dome of the Rock') : Built by the Caliph Omar on the site of the Temple at Jerusalem, around the Rock from which Mohammed was said to have ascended to heaven. Jerusalem was a Holy City and centre of pilgrimage to Muslims as well as to Jews and Christians.

Muezzin : The official of the mosque who ascends the minaret to make the Profession of Faith and the Call to Prayer at the five Muslim prayer-times of the day.

Order : A monastic rule of life, and hence a body of men living by that rule. Also used of the degrees of the clergy, e.g., 'Holy Orders' and 'Minor Orders'

Orthodox Church : (Literally 'of right doctrine' : c.f., Catholic—'universal'). The Greek form of Christianity which diverged from the Western form after the fall of the Roman Empire and finally broke with Rome in 1054. Apart from differences of doctrine and practice the Greek Church, unlike the Roman, remained closely connected with and subject to the Imperial authority. It remained so when it was adopted by Russia. Bulgaria and Serbia were also converted from Constantinople, and the alphabet used today by all these countries is a modified form of the Greek alphabet introduced by Orthodox missionaries.

Ottoman Turks : A line of Turkish rulers taking their name from the founder Othman, who in the fourteenth century made themselves dominant in Western Asia Minor and then absorbed the remains of the Byzantine Empire, making Constantinople their capital in 1453. They remained rulers of Turkey till the end of the First World War.

Sergeants : From Latin *servientes*, literally 'servants'. Originally infantry subordinate to the knights, then fully-armed as distinct from irregular infantry, and in later times leaders of infantry subordinate to officers.

Slavs : A group of peoples of similar language and origin, including the Russians, Poles, Lithuanians, Czechs, and Jugoslavs.

Tactics : Methods of employing troops in battle, as distinct from strategy, the art of moving armies into favourable positions for attack or defence.

Timurlane : (1336–1405). A Mongol ruler who conquered most of Central Asia, Persia, and Syria, invaded India, and defeated the Turks near Ankara. At his death he was marching to conquer China. The hero of the Elizabethan dramatist Marlowe's *Tamburlaine*.

True Cross : Believed to have been discovered on Mount Calvary by the Empress Helena (mother of Constantine) in A.D. 326, and since preserved in Jerusalem. Fragments purporting to come from it were sold in Mediaeval Europe in great quantities as relics.

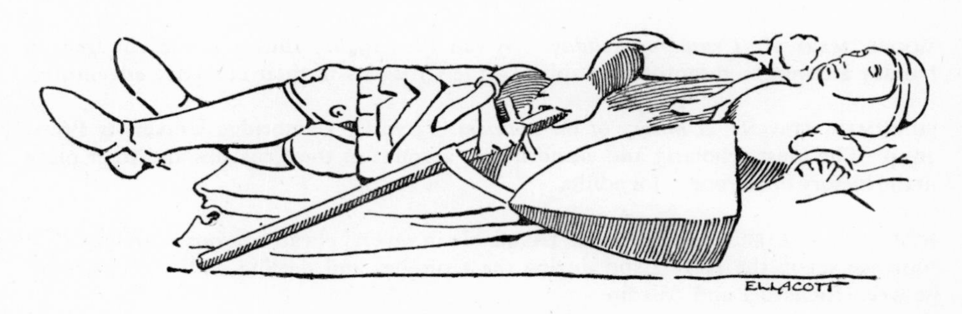

A Crusader's Tomb-Effigy:
Mauger St. Aubyn, d. 1294,
Georgeham,
Devon

A SELECT BOOK LIST

By Elizabeth N. Bewick, A.L.A.

BAKER, GEORGE. *Lionheart : the story of Richard Cœur De Lion.* Lutterworth. 1954. Maps. A vivid account of the life and exploits of Richard I, crusader, and King of England, 1189–1199.

CALDER, JEAN MCKINLAY. *The story of nursing.* Methuen's Outlines. 1954. Illus. A history of the growth of the nursing profession, including the development of the religious and military nursing orders of crusading times.

MOORE, MARY F. *Crusading holiday.* Sylvan Pr. 1946. Illus. Three children on holiday attempt to recapture the spirit of the Crusades in their everyday adventures.

RUNCIMAN, STEVEN. *A history of the crusades.* (3 vols.) Cambridge University Press. 1954. The most scholarly and authoritative account of the Crusades and their place in the history of Europe : for adults.

SCOTT, SIR WALTER. *The Talisman.* (Available in several cheap editions.) An historical romance set in the Holy Land during the Crusades and dealing with the campaign between Richard I and Saladin.

SELLMAN, R. R. *Castles and fortresses.* Methuen's Outlines. 1954. Illus. Maps. Diagrams. The history of western fortification from prehistoric to modern times.

TOY, SIDNEY. *Castles : a short history of fortifications from* 1600 B.C. *to* A.D. 1600. Heinemann. 1939. Illus. The development of the art of fortification with particular reference to Europe and the Levant.

WELCH, RONALD. *Knight crusader.* O.U.P. 1954. Illus. An historical adventure story of Philip d'Aubigny, knight crusader, and his exploits in the Holy Land.

WILMOT-BUXTON, E. M. *The story of the Crusades.* ("Told through the ages" series.) Harrap. Illus. The story of 200 years of the Holy War between Christians and Saracens for the possession of Jerusalem.

INDEX

Figures in italics refer to maps